One Young Fool In Dorset

Me with my mother - 1955

Victoria Twead

New York Times and Wall Street Journal Bestselling Author

One Young Fool in Dorset is the prequel
to the 'Old Fools' series.
Also available in Large Print and e-Book editions.

The Old Fools Series
Victoria Twead

- One Young Fool in Dorset: The Prequel
- Chickens, Mules and Two Old Fools (Wall Street Journal Bestseller)
- Two Old Fools ~ Olé!
- Two Old Fools on a Camel (New York Times Bestseller x 3)
- Two Old Fools in Spain Again

In loving memory of Jean and Frank.

And with heartfelt thanks to Annabel who shared
her parents with me so unselfishly.

❀ ❀ ❀

*Older sister,
little brother
and me*

Contents

Childhood and Dorset Recipes

1
Knickers and Rats

Perhaps I'm two years old, maybe less. There is a garden, and two big strong legs. The legs belong to Lena, our German nanny. A wicker laundry basket sits beside me. I'm not interested in the legs. Neither do I care about the wicker basket. I'm far too busy marvelling at the perfectly spherical little balls I'm finding in the grass. I amuse myself by collecting a pile. I pick them up and drop them. They roll down the bank. I taste one. It isn't nice.

"She's playing with rabbit droppings," pipes a voice above me. My big sister. "And now she's eating them."

Lena swipes the little balls from my chubby grasp. I howl, but not for long. There is always something else to explore.

❋ ❋ ❋

Now I'm four and play in the front more than the back, sharing toys with neighbouring kids. We live in a leafy cul-de-sac lined with white houses, each identical to its neighbour. There are tall pine trees where red squirrels twitch and dance. Our quiet street opens onto a bigger, much busier road, noisy with traffic. Sometimes a big black limousine, with a Union Jack flag fixed to the bonnet, passes by. White motorcycles, ridden by men dressed in white uniforms, surround the limousine.

"There's somebody important in that black car," says my big sister.

My sister is four years older than me and already knows stuff. She is clever and her hair is straight and shiny. Mine is unruly and points in all directions.

"Wer?" I ask in German. "Who?"

"I don't know, but those men on motorcycles are called the White Rats."

I watch, fascinated, until the convoy passes.

It is Germany in the late 1950s and we are stationed in Bonn because my father is an officer in the Army.

"We're going to help at the cocktail party tonight," says my sister, when the convoy has passed. "We'll wear our party dresses and carry trays. Lena says you can help, too."

I like that idea. My sister has been helping at cocktail parties for ages, but I'm always told I'm too young. This will be my first cocktail party. I like my party dress. It is swishy and white with puffed sleeves, a blue sash and a stiff lacy petticoat.

Cocktail parties at our house happen often. I sense that my parents dislike them but they are necessary because of the Army. Days beforehand, Lena polishes the silver and sweeps the carpets until everything is spotless. My mother is distracted and edgy. It all has to be perfect. My father looks handsome, resplendent in his dress uniform, his moustache bristling.

Upstairs, Lena sponges us down and wipes our faces and hands.

"Just a lick and a promise today," she says in German, "there's so much to do. Now, go and make a start on getting dressed. Thank goodness your baby brother is asleep."

Our clothes are laid out on our beds. My sister and I dress ourselves as far as we can, petticoat first, then dresses. I can't manage the buckles on my party shoes or the many buttons down the back of my party dress. I toddle off to find Lena.

"You've done well," she says, adjusting my white socks so that they are the right way round, buckling my shoes and buttoning the dress. "Now you can go downstairs and hand out nibbles when the guests arrive. Just for half an hour, mind. Now, out of my way, and don't mess up your dress."

I don't follow her all the way down. I sit on the stairs and watch the final preparations through the bannisters. How pretty Mummy looks with lipstick! How the sherry decanters sparkle on the sideboard!

The doorbell rings, and Lena hurries away to open the door to the guests.

Gradually, the room fills up with ladies who screech with laughter and wear jewellery that flashes signals when the light catches it. Their husbands stand tall in their uniforms, deep in conversation with each other. My sister carries a tray and weaves in and out through the knots of people, pausing to offer dainty nibbles. My mother wears a painted-on lipstick smile. At first, I can hear her making conversation using her brittle telephone voice, then, as the room fills and the noise level rises to a continuous buzz, I can no longer make out individual voices.

"Victoria! There you are!" Lena grabs my arm and helps me down the stairs and into the throng. "Don't be shy! Take this bowl and offer it to the guests. Just like your sister is doing."

I like the way my party dress rustles and swishes. I walk though the haze of perfume and forest of legs, then stop and hold my bowl up. Perhaps my sister has already done her job too well, because nobody takes any. I move on. Even when I tap on legs, the guests barely notice me.

I set the bowl carefully back on the sideboard. Now I just meander between the clusters of people, listening to the buzz, the sudden brays of laughter, hypnotised by the rustle of my own skirts. I lift my party dress to see the lacy petticoat beneath. Then I lift that, too.

"Lena! Victoria has no knickers on! And she's showing *everybody!*"

Strong German arms whisk me away and I am put to bed. The party is over for me and Lena resolves to supervise my dressing more closely in future.

❆ ❆ ❆

I was born in 1955, in Dorchester in the UK, the nearest hospital to Bovington Army Camp where my father was stationed. The hospital, built in 1841 from local Portland stone, has now been converted to flats, but still looks much the same as it always did. I only just managed to be born on British soil because six months later our family was sent to Bonn. My sister was already four years old and my brother was destined to be born two years later. I was the peanut butter in the middle of the sandwich.

My mother, big sister and me at Bovington

Only ghosts of memories stay with me when I think of those first five years in Germany. Being Austrian, my mother's first language was German, although she was fluent in English, too. Lena, our nanny, spoke only German. My father, although English, spoke good German. I grew up knowing only German, but my sister, who was now at the army school, was already bilingual.

I remember there were monkeys at the petrol station. I always begged Lena to walk that way so that we could see the monkeys in the cage. As we passed, the monkeys leapt from one side to the other, making the cage rattle alarmingly.

I remember walking beside Lena as she pushed my newborn brother in a huge pram alongside the river Rhine. The water was brown and the river was so big I could hardly see the other side. Dirty waves lapped at the bank. I licked at my ice cream until, horror, the cone crumbled in my hand and the ice cream splatted on the cement path. I opened my mouth to howl, but stopped when a dachshund popped up from nowhere and lapped the path clean with a few deft licks from his pink tongue.

I recall taking a ferry across the Rhine to go to kindergarten. At Christmas, I remember a wonderful cardboard structure on a table in the classroom. It was like a church but with turrets, battlements and windows with arched shutters. Each little window was numbered and we children took it in turns to open a set of cardboard shutters every day to reveal a stained-glass window made from coloured tissue paper. Candles had been lit inside the structure. It was the first Advent calendar I had ever seen, and still remains the most beautiful. I suspect it must have been a huge fire hazard and would certainly have never passed today's stringent health and safety rules.

Later, I think I was also sent for a short time to an army-organised preschool group, where only English was spoken. I understood very little that the teacher said. I wasn't happy because one of the rules was that you had to ask permission to leave the room if you were going to sneeze. I was terrified that a sneeze might sneak up on me, unannounced, before I had time to ask permission to leave the room. And what was the point of saying 'Present' when my name was called in the morning? That present never materialised.

Our car was a black Rover 90 and my sister said it belonged to the Queen. Apparently we were just borrowing it.

Most of my memories of Germany are mere snatches. Like the terrifying person called *Schwarz Peter* (Black Peter) who carried a small whip and followed St. Nicholas (Father Christmas) looking for bad children to punish; eating yoghurt from glass jars with long spoons; the children's book *Der Struwwelpeter* (Shockheaded Peter) which showed a boy who never cut his hair or nails, a cautionary tale to scare young children; and staring curiously at the floppy thing the boy next door kept in his underpants and insisted on showing me whenever he had the opportunity.

When I was five, the family returned to Dorset, England, leaving Lena behind. But my parents refused to stay in Army quarters this time, and the search began for 'the perfect house'.

Throughout their lives, my parents never decided anything in a hurry.

They researched, discussed and deliberated over every decision. So when it came to buying a house, they were cautious. They refused to rush into a purchase, and wisely decided to rent a property until the perfect house came along.

"*Ach,* I've always dreamed of living in a little *olde worlde* English cottage, with a thatched roof and cottage garden," said my mother with stars in her eyes.

And that's exactly what they found.

The picturesque village of Corfe Castle is dominated by the ruined thousand-year-old castle built by William the Conquerer, a magnet to visitors who gasp as they snap pictures with their cameras. The castle stands on a hill, with the village in its shadow.

Corfe Castle

If one walks along East Street from the Greyhound pub at the village centre, before one reaches the Purbeck stone-built village school, there is a row of thatched cottages on the left. The houses are terraced, shouldering each other like square beads on a necklace. One of them was available to rent.

"Well, it's certainly *olde worlde,*" said my father.

"I love it!" said my mother. "I wonder how old it is?"

"Very handy for the school," said my father. "It's just steps away. Not even a road to cross."

"*Ach,* this is *exactly* the kind of house I'd like us to find for ourselves to buy," my mother trilled, in raptures. "Very old, with *heaps* of character."

We moved in, but we weren't the only residents. We were sharing the house with spiders, mice and rats, all of whom regarded the thatched roof and its surrounds as their home. Very quickly, my mother decided she didn't want to live in an *olde worlde* property after all.

The school was very handy for me, although I remember almost nothing about it. My sister, however, was attending a preparatory school in Dorchester, and needed to catch a train. The train station backed onto our cottage garden and my father, ever ingenious, constructed a ladder for my sister to scale the wall at the bottom of the garden. Every day, dressed in her school uniform with her satchel on her back, she would climb the ladder and catch the huffing steam train waiting at the platform. The stationmaster was fully aware of this arrangement, which suited everybody.

My sister must have been a familiar little figure, because one day, she was late and the train had already drawn away from the platform, leaving her behind. But the engine driver must have caught sight of her, because he stopped the train, then shunted back to pick her up.

Corfe Castle railway station

Corfe had its own railway station until 1972 when British Rail closed both station and the line. Luckily there were plenty of passionate railway enthusiasts around, and the station and line reopened in August 1995 as a heritage line. The old steam trains puff in and out once more, this time carrying tourists instead of taking children to school and folks to work.

Meanwhile, my parents drove us around the countryside, estate agents' details in hand, as they scoured the towns and villages of Dorset for the perfect home.

They had a check list which included a decent-sized garden, enough bedrooms for all of us, and a location not too far from Bovington Army Camp where my father would be working. Houses with thatched roofs, which before might have sent my mother swooning, were now firmly struck off the viewing list.

Weekends were spent house hunting, and all the towns and villages within a twenty-five mile radius were explored. During the week, my father would spread a map on the floor and, armed with the latest estate agents' blurbs, he and my mother would plan the route.

"There's one here," said my father, tapping the town marked 'Wareham' on the map.

My mother squinted at one of the estate agent papers in her hand.

"*Ach*, I saw that one," she said, "but that house looked very dilapidated."

"But Wareham is a nice town," my father insisted. "Look, it's right on the river, in fact it has a quay. And I know the Saxon walls still stand. I'll talk to the estate agent. I think this house might be worth a visit."

My mother, who loved history, added the house to the viewing list but pencilled in a question mark.

The village of Corfe Castle is exactly halfway between the bustling market town of Wareham and the popular seaside resort of Swanage, so it wasn't too far to drive to Wareham that weekend. We sailed over the pretty white bridge that spanned the river and admired the quay. Two swans glided on the river, followed by their family of cygnets.

"Can we stop here?" we begged, but my father ignored our pleas.

"Slow down, this is it," said my mother, peering out of the window.

"Do we *have* to go and look at another house?" we children moaned.

By now, even my parents had almost despaired of finding the perfect property, and they didn't hold out much hope for this particular house either.

My father parked, and we all stared out of the car windows. The *For Sale* sign had lurched drunkenly sideways and was choked by weeds, sending the message that the house had been on the market for a long time. The house itself was big, rather ugly, square and solid.

"*Ach*, I don't hold out much hope for this one," said my mother.

The front of the house might have looked even worse, but being springtime, it was softened by a cluster of apple trees in full blossom, their roots obscured by long grass and bluebells. Already crazy about animals and wildlife, I imagined what birds I might see, and whether dormice would come and nibble the fallen apples in autumn.

"Well, this is definitely the house," said my father. "I don't know why, but the estate agent was reluctant for us to see this one, he didn't think it would suit us at all. The owner should be expecting us. Let's knock on the door."

We climbed out of the car and walked up the weed-choked drive. The house was pebble-dashed, although many of the pebbles had fallen away leaving bald yellow patches. The drainpipes and guttering hung at crazy angles.

My mother and we three children stood back as my father pushed through the overgrown bushes to reach the peeling front door.

He knocked.

2
Priests and Pets

"Sssh," said my father, listening.

I could hear little birds, and bees busy in the apple blossom, but nobody came to the door. He tried knocking again, but there was no response.

"*Ach,* this door doesn't look as though it's been used for a long time," said my mother. "Shall we try the back door?"

We all traipsed round to the back door, and my father tried again.

Dogs barked within. The birds in the apple trees sang as we stood stock still, listening. At last, somebody fumbled with locks.

"Curse this door! Be'jeesus if the blessed thing ain't banjaxed..."

Even at the age of six, I knew the man behind the door spoke in a strange way.

"Mummy, why does he talk all funny?" I piped up.

"Sssh, he's Irish, a Roman Catholic priest."

That meant nothing to me.

The door finally swung back, revealing the occupier of the house.

"Ah, an' ye'll be the family come to see me house?"

The man framed in the doorway had tufts of unruly white hair attached to an otherwise bald head. His shapeless ears seemed huge, and his face was as red as the tomatoes Lena used to chop. Several day's growth of white bristles sprouted from his mottled skin. His nose was bulbous and as shapeless as a potato. He wore a threadbare cassock, once black, now blotched with food stains down the front, the fabric grey with age. I stared at him, then into the house behind him, but it was too dark to make out anything.

My father stepped forward to shake hands, but the priest drew back, one hand on the doorknob, the other clutching the large crucifix dangling round his neck.

"Welcome to me humble abode," he said and waved us in.

We trouped into the dark interior. The smell of stale cigarettes and cooked cabbage hung in the air. The windows were so nicotine-stained and filthy that very little light penetrated. Bare, low-wattage lightbulbs hung down in the centre of most rooms, but few of them worked. Great slices of yellowed wallpaper hung from the walls where they'd come unstuck.

"Where's the furniture?" I asked as we were taken from one room to another.

"Shhh..." said my mother.

One room was filled with potatoes. In another, a ramshackle bed leaned in the corner. The sheets were grey, the blankets peppered with round cigarette burns. Above it, a wooden crucifix was nailed to the wall, Jesus sporting a broken nose.

"Me bedroom," said the priest, and then stopped at another door. "And this room here is where me dogs sleep."

There was scratching of large claws on the door, and deep excited woofs.

"That's okay," said my father hurriedly. "Don't disturb them."

"Ye may be right," chuckled our host. "There's t'ree of 'em, Matthew, Mark and Luke. Used ter have four, y'know, praise the Lord, but John passed on. They're big Oirish wolfhounds, so they are. They'll probably be knockin' yer yunguns over so we'll leave 'em be."

"Mummy? Why isn't there any carpet or lino on the floor?" I asked as we continued down the hall.

"Shhh…" said my mother.

"And why does it smell funny?"

Exasperated, my mother turned to our guide.

"*Ach*, Father, may we send the children outside into the garden to explore?" she asked. "We can join them later when we've been upstairs. If that's okay with you, of course?"

"Of course!" he said, bending down to my level. "Pr'aps ye'll find some little people in the garden, so ye will."

"Little people?" I asked, wilting under the blast of foul breath directed straight into my face.

"Leprechauns, fairies, you know…" said my sister, the clever one.

Now, that was interesting! We exploded out of the back door into the bright light.

The back garden was a tangled wilderness. Brambles and stinging nettles vied with each other and it was difficult to identify any boundaries. Ivy strangled trees and fences. The garden had no lawns and the paths were merely ones flattened by the priest's feet. I could see it was the perfect place to build dens and hide with a book. Even at that age, I was the quiet one, the loner, the one who preferred to sit in a wardrobe looking at books rather than play with the others.

"Mummy says the grounds are a third of an acre," said my sister. "And I don't believe in little people."

I didn't care what size the grounds were and, whatever my big sister said, I was sure little people could be found, if one looked hard enough.

I loved the garden and tiptoed around searching. I saw no fairies, no pixies, no little people, but I didn't give up hope. There were so many places I could crouch unseen, watching insects while weaving stories in my mind. I

16

climbed an apple tree.

All too soon, my parents emerged from the house and called us.

"Kids! Come on, we're going home now."

They didn't say a word until my father started the engine and the car drew away.

"It's a mess," said my father.

"It would take *years* to get that house straight," said my mother.

"All the electrics need stripping out completely. That place is a fire hazard."

"And the smell!"

"Can you believe he has a room for potatoes and another for his dogs?"

"*Ach,* and that kitchen! And did you see how overgrown the garden was?"

They both paused, staring through the windscreen, lost in their thoughts.

"I can see why it's been on the market for so long," said my father, but his eyes were gleaming.

"I loved the garden!" I piped up, but nobody heard me.

Even at the grand old age of six, I could read between the lines. The more my parents criticised and found fault with the house, the more sure I was that they were going to buy it. This strange house with the smelly rooms and tangled garden would be our new home.

And I was right. Negotiations were soon completed and we prepared to move out of the rented, thatched, rat-ridden Corfe Castle cottage, and into the house that would be our home until all three of us children spread our adult wings and flew the nest.

The end of the summer term approached, the last of my time at Corfe village school. I was presented with a prize. Was it for producing excellent schoolwork? I'm afraid not. I daydreamed all through my schooling then, and would continue to do so at all the centres of education I attended. No, the prize was for becoming fluent in English during the six months I was there. Hardly surprising really; nobody spoke German at Corfe Castle village school.

"I want the bedroom that looks down on the apple trees and bluebells," said my sister.

Being the eldest, she was given her first choice. In fact, I ended up with the best room. My window overlooked the garden, and was the biggest bedroom, apart from that of my parents. In the next few years, the apple trees at the front of the house were chopped down, and the bluebells and primroses were paved over to create space for car parking, so the view from my sister's bedroom window became very dull.

That summer, I ran wild in the garden of our new house. Much of it was brambles, but before my parents had a chance to tame it, I made dens and secret hidey-holes where I could look at books in peace, without my annoying little brother finding me.

My mother had always dreamed of having her own garden. Instead of books, she read seed merchants' leaflets and every windowsill was crowded with little pots and emerging seedlings. Gardening books like *The Art of Propagation* and *Growing Vegetables* began to appear on the bookshelves. I know that she spent a great deal of time designing the layout of the garden and deciding what to plant. The bottom half was to be given over to vegetables, whilst the top part was going to be laid to lawn with a terrace for a table and chairs.

In the early days, my mother nearly despaired of that garden because it wasn't merely weeds she was digging up. As she forked the soil, the prongs clattered against glass.

"*Ach,* not another one!" she said as she drew out a whiskey bottle and added it to the growing pile.

Dorset Apple Cake

A very easy recipe, great for using up fallen cooking apples. Fantastic with custard.

110g (4 oz) margarine or butter
225g (8 oz) flour
110g (4 oz) sugar
55g (2 oz) currants
225g (8 oz) chopped apple
A little milk

Method
- Rub fat into flour and add sugar, currants and apple.
- Mix together with milk to make a stiff dough.
- Spoon mixture into a greased round cake tin.
- Cook in a hot oven (220C/430F/ Gas 7) for 10 minutes then turn down the heat to 170C/335F/Gas 3 and cook for a further hour.

The previous owner, the Roman Catholic priest, clearly had a problem. Because of his standing in the community, he probably felt it wise to keep evidence of his secret vice hidden. Instead of throwing his empty whiskey bottles out with the trash, he buried them in the garden. My mother unearthed so many that she lost count. Now *we* had inherited the problem of disposing of these bottles. Would the dustbin men think *we* were alcoholics and spread rumours around town?

"*Ach,* I don't care what people think of us," said my mother, and for weeks the whiskey bottles clattered into our dustbin.

Eventually she dug up the last one. I imagine the bin men thought we were miraculously cured because no more bottles filled our dustbin.

Of course, summer couldn't last for ever, although as a child one thinks it will. I had a new school to attend, and a difficult act to follow; my big sister.

My sister was very bright and shone at all her school subjects without even trying. I wasn't stupid, but I was lazy when it came to school work. I lived in a daydream and was happiest in my own company, reading books or writing my own stories. I still have my first masterpiece.

the runaway tadel
wunce there was a runaway tadel and when
you put food on it it ran away the end.

My sister already attended the little preparatory school in Dorchester, and it was decided that I should join her there.

The school was in a residential street, a building several floors high, as I remember. There was a flight of steps and the headmistress, Mrs Pellow, stood at the top to welcome the new children. She was a big woman and I was terrified.

"Ah," she said, "I recognise the family resemblance! Do you have a big sister in the school? A very clever big sister?"

I nodded, my eyes huge with fright. I was too scared to speak. She reached towards me and clasped me to her ample bosom. It felt like I had sunk into a vast feather pillow, and although it wasn't unpleasant, I was afraid I might suffocate.

"Hello Victoria, and welcome," she said, eventually releasing me. "Did you know that the nicest things come in small parcels?"

I didn't. I greedily gulped in air.

School was to be endured, a necessary evil that had to be sat through until the doors finally opened and we could escape. At break times we played in the small playground, boys one side, girls the other. The days were long because we had to catch the train from Wareham station, then walk to school in a group supervised by a teacher. The summer holidays seemed to be just out of reach.

"Now," said our teacher on the last day of term, "While you are away, I want you all to write a composition of what you did during the holidays. Bring it with you in September, when school starts again, and the best ones will receive prizes."

"Do we *have* to do it?" asked a classmate.

"No, but you can't win a prize if you don't enter."

I knew I could never win, and I had no competitive spirit anyway, so I never did write that composition. Instead I spent the summer in the garden catching woodlice and trying to train them to do tricks.

"Now, it's only a little twig, I want you to jump it."

But the woodlouse simply stood stock still, or rolled into a ball like an armadillo.

"Okay, just climb over it. If you do, I promise to find you some *delicious* rotten wood to eat."

However nicely I asked, it refused to obey my commands.

I kept records of the birds that visited our garden, but it wasn't enough. I was desperately wanted a pet of my own, but my pleas fell on deaf ears.

"Mummy, please, please, please, please, please can I have a pet?"

"*Ach,* it's out of the question."

"Why?"

"Because I said so."

"Why can't I have a pony?"

"*Ach,* where would we keep a pony?"

"Well, a dog, then? Just a little puppy?"

"Puppies grow into dogs. They need looking after, and walks. And who would end up looking after it? Muggins here, of course."

"What about a kitten? They don't need walks."

"Kittens grow into cats, and cats will chase all the birds out of our garden."

"I could train it not to."

"You can't train cats not to catch birds."

"Well, what about a guinea pig? They don't chase birds."

"You wouldn't look after it."

"I would, I *promise* I would…"

"No, it's out of the question."

No amount of sulks, tears or pouting would change their minds.

I dreamed of having a pony. I dreamed of having a puppy. Owning a pet filled my thoughts. I probably drove my family insane.

Until one day, when I was given a box.

"It's a pet," said my father. "We decided that because your school report wasn't too bad, perhaps you deserve a pet."

My school report had just arrived in the post. It was probably the best one I ever received and I'm pretty sure my teachers were lenient because I'd only just joined the school.

❊ ❊ ❊

School Report
Reading: Victoria is making steady progress.
Writing: Victoria is developing a good style.
Oral Composition: Good, although shy.
Written Composition: Victoria enjoys this and has made progress.
Arithmetic: Could do better.
Nature Study: Excellent.

❊ ❊ ❊

Inside the cardboard box was a tortoise. In those days, tortoises were freely available in pet shops, and the fact that huge numbers died as they were shipped abroad, packed on top of each other without food and water, was of little consequence.

It wasn't quite the pet I had in mind. I couldn't take this pet for walks on a leash. Nevertheless, I was delighted with Timmy the tortoise. My father built a run for him with a little hutch one end where he could retreat during inclement weather. I fed him pieces of tomato and banana which he crushed in his toothless mouth. I found him juicy dandelion leaves and sometimes lifted him out of the run and let him explore the garden.

By now, my mother was getting to grips with the unruly garden and was no longer digging up whiskey bottles. Whilst creating lawns, new flowerbeds, laying paths and raising vegetables, she was slowly discovering the passion of her life: gardening.

I couldn't understand how a short stroll to drop some potato peelings on the compost heap at the bottom of the garden could take her half an hour. But it did because she had to pause to smell the buddleia flowers, or admire the cyclamen seedlings which unwound like springs, or check if baby lettuce had pushed through the soil overnight. I didn't understand the attraction until twenty years later when I, too, had my first garden and my own passion for gardening was born.

The garden was already unrecognisable, bearing no resemblance to the one we inherited. We now had a paved terrace on which I would later

---

Dorset Herby Potato Salad

The many hours of sunshine and mild temperatures of Dorset produce wonderfully tender early vegetables. This recipe uses tiny new potatoes, best cooked the same day as they are dug up.

Serves 4 - 6

700g (1½ lb) small new potatoes
2 hard-boiled egg yolks
Large pinch of cayenne pepper
5ml (1 tsp) caster sugar
1 tbsp chopped fresh herbs, perhaps tarragon, chives, mint or parsley
15ml (1 tbsp) herb vinegar
150ml (5 fl oz) natural yoghurt or sour cream
Snipped fresh chives, to garnish

Method
- Wash the potatoes, but don't peel. Cook in boiling salted water for 10-15 minutes, until tender.
- Meanwhile, make the dressing by mashing the egg yolks, cayenne pepper and sugar to a paste with the chopped herbs, the vinegar and 1 tsp cold water.
- Stir in the yoghurt.
- When the potatoes are cooked, drain thoroughly and toss with the dressing while still warm, even if you intend to serve the dish cold, as the dressing will distribute better.
- Serve either warm or cold, garnished with snipped chives.

21

learn to roller skate. There was a little wall built from yellow Purbeck stone in front of which giant gaudy African marigolds stood in battalions. Clumps of lavender scented the air, edging a lawn big enough to put up a badminton net.

As she forked, dug and planted, my mother would enter a kind of trance. This could be useful because it was the perfect opportunity should I want to raid the larder or get up to any mischief. I could time my misdeeds carefully, knowing that if she was busy gardening, she would never notice anything.

As my mother laboured happily in the garden, she would often collect Timmy the tortoise and place him in the middle of the lawn. Timmy meandered around, munching contentedly on daisies. Tortoises aren't known for their speed, but Timmy regularly surprised us by sprinting to the edge of the lawn and diving into a flowerbed when our backs were turned.

"He's gone again."

"Oh no, did you see which direction he was heading?"

If we stood still and watched the flowerbeds, we'd see a clump of flowers shaking, or being roughly pushed aside.

"Timmy! There you are!" I squealed.

Usually he wasn't difficult to find and we'd soon scoop him up and return him to the centre of the lawn.

Of course it was bound to happen. One day, while my mother was absorbed in her garden, she forgot all about Timmy. By the time she remembered him, he'd vanished.

"When did you last see him?"

"*Ach,* I'm not sure… It was probably when I was planting the artichokes. Perhaps an hour ago…"

"An hour?"

At first we didn't worry, but when he didn't appear all afternoon, thorough searches were organised. It was a big garden, much of it still untamed. As we searched, our arms were scratched by brambles and our knees were muddied, but there was no sign of Timmy.

Night fell, and Timmy was still missing.

I cried myself to sleep.

3
Jeannie and Beach Days

My mother didn't want us to have pets, and she didn't like dogs much. When I asked her why, she said it was because *her* mother bred dogs. That sounded like a reason to *like* dogs, not dislike them. I really didn't understand, but her mother and dogs were topics she refused to talk about, so I regretfully accepted the state of affairs.

We children never met our grandmother or grandfather. It wasn't until I was nearly sixty years old and living in Spain that we discovered the jaw-dropping secret my mother took to her grave. Until then, we didn't know what became of our grandfather, or why my mother wouldn't speak of our grandmother, or her own childhood. But that's another story which I saved for the fourth *Old Fools* book.

However, there were two canine exceptions to my mother's rule. She actually *liked* two particular dogs. One was Sam, a border collie belonging to our friends, the Hale family, who owned a large country estate on the other side of Wareham. Sam was grumpy and known to bite, which terrified me, but I knew that he was astonishingly intelligent. He was a trained sheep dog and knew what was needed even before his master did. He could even open gates.

The other exception was beautiful Jeannie.

About six houses down the road from our house lived Mrs Cox, and her dog Jeannie. Mrs Cox was retired, but she used to be a professional photographer, and she had devoted much of her life to raising money for guide dogs for the blind. Jeannie was a golden retriever, and was being trained as a guide dog until she displayed a fear of manhole covers. Obviously her guide dog training couldn't continue. She never made the grade and was adopted by Mrs Cox instead.

Jeannie was friendly, happy, and obedient. She was gentle and loved everybody. Even my mother couldn't help herself and was fond of Jeannie.

At breakfast, the morning after we'd lost Timmy the tortoise, I was still miserable. My mother suddenly spoke up.

"What about Jeannie?" she said.

"Jeannie? Mrs Cox's dog Jeannie?" asked my father. "What about her?"

"You know how clever she is? And she's a retriever, yes?"

"Of course."

"*Ach*, why don't we ask Mrs Cox to bring Jeannie round here and see if they can find Timmy?"

"Worth a try, I suppose, but I don't hold out much hope."

My father was doubtful but I was ecstatic. I was *sure* clever Jeannie would find Timmy.

Later that morning, we all traipsed round to Mrs Cox's house and my mother explained the situation.

"I think Jeannie and I might be able to help," said Mrs Cox, one hand on Jeannie's soft head. "Let's go round to your place and see what we can do."

Back in our garden, we stood and watched.

Mrs Cox took Jeannie to Timmy's run. She lifted the roof off Timmy's little house and Jeannie snuffled the straw inside, her feathery tail lashing in wide sweeps. Then she looked up at Mrs Cox for instructions.

"Jeannie, go find it!"

Jeannie flew down the garden path and bounded onto the lawn. We all followed at a run.

"Go find it!" repeated Mrs Cox, panting.

Jeannie zigzagged across the lawn, nose down, tail high. We trailed her. At the lawn's edge, she paused and looked up at her mistress as though asking for permission.

"Jeannie, go find it!" said Mrs Cox.

Jeannie plunged into the flowerbed and I heard my mother's sharp intake of breath as her precious plants were pushed aside. Jeannie weaved her way through and out the other side. With her wet, black nose inches from the ground, Jeannie continued down another path, along the side of a hedge, then paused at my mother's compost heap.

The compost heap was a giant box constructed by my father with slats of wood. In very cold weather you could see it steaming. On warm days I sometimes saw slow-worms (harmless legless lizards, not worms at all) sunning themselves on top.

We all stopped, a little out of breath. Jeannie was panting now, pink tongue lolling, tail swishing hard and fast. She gave a low *woof* and waited for Mrs Cox to speak.

"Does Jeannie know where Timmy is?" I asked.

"I think so," said Mrs Cox. "Jeannie, go find it!"

Jeannie gave another deep *woof* and disappeared behind the compost heap. We waited, but not for long. Within moments, Jeannie backed out, feathery tail waving like a triumphant flag. In her soft mouth was Timmy.

"She found him!" I squealed.

Jeannie walked over to Mrs Cox and sat down in front of her. She was so gentle, and her mouth was so soft, that Timmy hadn't even withdrawn into his shell. His legs were still waving indignantly, pedalling the air.

"Good girl, Jeannie!" said Mrs Cox. "Drop it. Leave. Good girl."

Obediently, Jeannie set Timmy down. Timmy, relieved to have solid ground under his feet, set off again.

"Oh, no you don't," I said, and grabbed my athletic pet.

Jeannie was the heroine of the day and was rewarded with hugs, praise, and a bowl of cold water. An unrepentant Timmy was replaced in his run to plot his next break for freedom.

My brother, Jeannie and me

❀ ❀ ❀

To a child, summer lasts for ever. Days were long and my brother and I were often sent to bed before the stars popped out, and before the glow worms lit their lamps in the grass. In the morning, I could run barefoot across the lawn, leaving a trail of zig-zag footprints in the dew. Soon, the sun rose high in the sky and dried the dew, leaving no sign of my crazy dance.

I checked the little fairy houses I had made with sticks and leaves in secret parts of the garden. Of course I didn't believe in fairies, I told myself, but just *in case* they existed, I'd give them nice houses to live in.

Summer also meant visits to the beautiful beaches of Dorset. In that part of the world, one is spoilt for choice. Lesser known beaches, like Dancing

Ledge and Chapman's Pool could only be reached after a walk of many miles across heathland and down farm tracks.

But it was worth it. These wonderfully wild beaches are unique. At Dancing Ledge there is a natural pool cut out of the rock, much like an infinity pool with a sea view. At the turn of the tide, the pool becomes a jacuzzi as the water churns. It was far too dangerous for us children to be allowed to swim, but there were still plenty of rock pools to explore. Sometimes we took big pieces of seaweed home and hung them from trees. Apparently they made good weather forecasters: slimy seaweed meant wet weather ahead, while crisp, dry seaweed meant sunny spells to come.

Another favourite was Worbarrow Bay with its ghost village which sent shivers down my spine and my imagination into overdrive. I stared past the ropes at the empty cottages where people used to live. In those days, the beach was only open to the public on rare occasions, and you couldn't enter the village of Tyneham at all. The reason for this was that the Army used the surrounding land for driving tanks and armoured vehicles, and the whole area was a firing range.

In 1943, the War Office commandeered the entire acreage, including the little village of Tyneham. The War Office declared that it needed the land, beach and village to carry out military manoeuvres. The residents of Tyneham had no choice. Every family was forced to pack up and leave, abandoning their homes, school, and church. It must have been a devastating time but they were promised they could return after the war was over.

But it wasn't to be. World War II ended, but in 1947 the Army placed a compulsory purchase order on the land, and the villagers were never allowed to return.

The ghost village of Tyneham still stands, though it has fallen into disrepair and is damaged by practice shell fire. The church and schoolhouse, however, are intact and are now museums, I am told. And something very good came out of the Army owning the land. Because it is largely left alone by humans, and not cultivated in any way, the land now supports rare plants, birds and wildlife.

Oh, the joy of living along the Jurassic coastline where fossils revealed themselves as though clamouring for attention. We often visited Kimmeridge Bay. The village of Kimmeridge is tiny and very picturesque. The estimated population in 2013 was just 90. But Kimmeridge is well worth a visit for two good reasons, both of which I loved as a child.

First, it had an awesome folly. Perched precariously on the cliff edge and overlooking the semi-circular bay, was the folly known as Clavell Tower, which inspired P.D. James's novel, *The Black Tower*.

Who built it, and why? I didn't know. I imagine the person who built it thought it would stand proudly for ever. Indeed, there used to be space for horse-drawn carriages to drive on the strip of land between folly and cliff edge. But the cliff was constantly being eroded by the weather and the sea below. The folly was now mere feet away from the edge of the cliff and in real danger of collapsing into the waves beneath. Every time we visited the bay, I checked to see whether the folly was still standing, or had collapsed into its inevitable watery grave.

Clavell Tower as it was

To my astonishment, I recently learned that the folly survived for many more years. Finally, in 2006, it was taken over by the Landmark Trust which rescues eccentric buildings and converts them into holiday homes. They dismantled Clavell Tower and re-erected it on a firmer foundation 82 feet further inland.

Now it looks almost the same as it did when I was a child, except that it's no longer ruined, or in danger, and boasts a stunning interior with four floors of beautifully styled rooms. I imagine a few days' stay in this spectacular building, surrounded by breath-taking views, with the waves breaking beneath the cliffs, would make a truly unforgettable holiday.

The second attraction for me was fossils. The shale at Kimmeridge is soft and constantly crumbling, making the finding of ammonites easy.

"I've found one!"

"Me too!"

"And me!"

Ammonites, with their characteristic ribbed, spiral shell are probably the most widely known fossil. These creatures lived in our seas some 240 million years ago, before they became extinct along with the dinosaurs. It was awesome to uncover such an ancient thing. The windowsill in my bedroom became cluttered with the ammonite fossils I had found. I could never bear to part with them, and I know they came with me when I moved to Spain forty years later. I haven't seen them for a long time; perhaps they are languishing in a box somewhere. Perhaps some future fossil hunter may come across them in decades to come and wonder how Dorset fossils could possibly be found in the mountains of southern Spain.

But sometimes we visited beaches simply because they were beautiful. Durdle Door is a perfect example of a stunning setting, and often used in films, including the unforgettable *Far From the Madding Crowd.*

Durdle Door

But my very favourite beach was much more ordinary, or so I thought when we first started visiting it.

My mother didn't enjoy driving. She refused to drive any car at all, even though she had passed her driving test many years earlier. Then one day, my father came home with an old ex-army Land Rover. It had a torn canvas roof that was rolled back and tied at various points.

"Get in," he said handing her the ignition key. "Turn the engine on, see how it feels."

"*Ach,* this is not so bad," she said. "I feel high, much safer than an ordinary car. If I scratch it, it wouldn't really matter, would it? And I like that the engine is loud because I can hear what I'm doing."

She crunched the gears to demonstrate. My father winced.

The Land Rover had seen better days and was badly in need of a coat of paint, so my mother bought some and opened the lid. She peered at it, then dipped in her paintbrush.

"This is supposed to be dark green!" she said, as she began painting. "*Ach,* never mind. It's not a bad colour. It's like variegated ivy leaves."

The name stuck, and Ivy joined the family.

We kids loved Ivy. There were no seats in the back. We just sat on the floor holding onto anything we could, slipping and sliding and landing in a tangled heap when Ivy sailed round bends. It was great fun.

Sometimes we'd get up early and my mother would drive us to some local fields where we picked mushrooms. Ivy's big tyres left tracks in the silver dew.

Of course Ivy was also the perfect vehicle to take to the beach. The nearest sandy beach where kids could dig, make sandcastles, and bathe safely, was Studland. I don't remember my father ever going, but I guess he was at work. We kids piled into Ivy, along with the towels and picnic boxes. My mother would grip the steering wheel so hard that her knuckles were snow-white and off we'd go. The canvas roof flapped, the wind roared in our ears, and Ivy's engine was so loud that we had to shout to each other, or talk in sign language. It was all part of the fun.

Looking back on it now, I'm surprised we never had an accident as my mother's driving was appalling. We kids didn't care, and as we bucked and stalled all the way to the beach, we sang *Ten Green Bottles* at the tops of our voices.

Studland Bay is renowned for its fine sand and expanse of sand dunes. Dorset has a great deal of precious heathland where the adder (or viper), and the rare smooth snake thrives. Studland's sand dunes were a refuge for these shy snakes. In all the years I went there, I never saw a single one.

Studland is also renowned for something else, but I didn't know that at the time.

My mother ignored the car park and set off into the dunes, gloating over the fact that Ivy, with her four-wheel-drive, could go places where standard cars couldn't. We could navigate over quite soft sand and my mother would crow with delight at the thought that lesser vehicles may get stuck in the dunes. Over the dunes we sailed, Ivy lurching dramatically, with us kids grabbing each other in an effort not to be bounced out of the back.

Then came the search for a good place to park. Luckily, there was heaps of parking choice, because my mother's aversion to reversing meant we had to find somewhere where she could circle when it was time to leave.

Out came the towels and swimming stuff. We also brought a bottle of homemade suntan lotion. It was a nasty concoction, 50% cooking oil and 50% vinegar, to rub into our skins making us smell like fish and chip shops. These were the days before the dangers of skin cancer were known.

Weighed down with buckets, spades and beach paraphernalia, my brother and I cantered down to the beach, leaving my mother and older sister to follow at a more sensible pace.

Once on the beach, if one looked to the left, one would see the Sandbanks ferry crossing back and forth. Look right, and you'd see the Old Harry Rocks. Old Harry and his wives are white chalk stacks and stumps, chiselled out by the ocean and time. Poor Old Harry regularly loses wives to the waves.

Old Harry Rocks

My brother and I built sand castles, sand boats and sand cars. We buried each other and chased in and out of the waves.

"Picnic is ready!" called my mother.

We ate sandwiches, then my mother produced a tin opener and big can of sliced peaches. We held out our plastic bowls into which she tipped a few peach slices which slid around like goldfish. Then came a dash of evaporated milk. Tinned peaches always remind me of those days at Studland beach, and I still adore evaporated milk.

I learned to swim at Studland. I was at that stage when I was nearly swimming, but too nervous to lift my feet off the ground. A complete stranger detached himself from his family group and walked over to me.

"Put your chin in there," he commanded, cupping his hand.

I was so shocked, I did so.

"Now lift your legs and kick. Don't worry, I won't let your head sink under water."

I did as I was told as my family watched. I kicked my legs - and I was swimming! I never saw the stranger again, but he did me a big favour.

Sometimes my brother and I would explore the dunes for a while.

"Don't go too far!" called my mother. "And if you see something suspicious, don't dig it up."

We knew what she meant. Studland had been used as a practice firing range at one time, and it wasn't unusual to unearth an unexploded shell.

On one particular occasion, perhaps that year or later, we went deep into the dunes. We were African explorers hunting big game. Sometimes we had to drop onto all-fours to hide from lions. Once, a giant python (well, a piece of discarded tubing) nearly grabbed us, but we were too fast. We rolled down the dune out of its reach. We crawled, commando-style, around a particularly large dune, utterly silent, then froze.

In front of us lay a group of adults sunbathing. They were a mixed bunch of men and ladies, stretched out on towels. Their eyes were closed and apart from a hand swishing away the odd fly, they didn't move.

But there was something astounding about these grown-ups that caused my brother and I to gape, then stare at each other with round, disbelieving eyes.

4
Naked

"They've got no clothes on!" I mouthed to my brother.

"They're bare!" he whispered, his eyes out on stalks.

We backed away, hands covering our mouths, eyes like manhole covers. I don't know why we were so shocked because both our parents often wandered around in the nude at home, and there were no locks on the bathroom door. They were totally uninhibited, and if it was hot, they took off their clothes. To them it was logical. We kids accepted that, but to see *other* people, in public, without clothes on, was most unexpected.

The quickest way back to our picnic party was along the beach. We pelted over the dunes, back to the normality of the beach, then froze.

Everyone was naked.

Family groups, children making sandcastles. Couples stretched out sunbathing. People paddling at the water's edge. Grandparents under sun shades, reading or dozing. Teenagers throwing balls or frisbees to each other.

They were all naked.

"We're the only ones with clothes on!"

Crimson with embarrassment and without looking left or right, we made a dash for it. Along the beach we galloped, not stopping until we reached our own beach party, who were decently clothed.

"Whatever is the matter with you two?" asked our sister.

"Back there..." I squeaked, clutching my chest and gasping for breath.

"*Ach,* what?" asked my mother.

"Back there..."

"Yes?"

"*Nobody has got any clothes on!*"

"They're all *bare!*" said my brother, whose eyebrows had disappeared into his hairline.

"*Ach,*" said my mother, not in the least concerned. "You wandered too far, that's all. You went as far as the naturist beach."

"Naturist?"

"Yes, some people prefer not to wear clothes at all. Did you not see the big blue warning signs?"

I thought hard. Yes, I'd seen the signs, but I thought naturists were people who liked nature and wildlife, like me. And I certainly didn't know that for decades, in fact since the 1920s, one kilometre of the beach had been given over to nudists. Studland is probably the best known naturist beach in Great Britain and is run by the National Trust.

Studland was a popular beach for naturists and families alike, and some summer days the cars queued for miles as families headed to the beach. Often they sat stationary, nose to tail, engines idling, baking in the sun as they waited to creep forward. This set my mother's brain ticking. She had an entrepreneurial spirit that constantly devised ways to make extra money.

"*Ach*, I'll go to Cash and Carry and buy Coca-Colas," she said. "Then I will park Ivy in a lay-by and I'll walk up and down the line of cars, selling Coca-Colas. I will make a fortune! They will be so thirsty and tired of queuing, they will definitely want to buy my drinks. *Ach*, I can't understand why nobody has thought of it before!"

"Are you sure you don't need a licence?" asked my father mildly.

"*Ach*, who would stop me selling a few cans of drink?"

My father made her a tray that she could carry, like cinema ice cream sellers, and the next hot weekend she loaded Ivy with cans of Coke. With a crunching of gears and cloud of exhaust fumes, she set off towards Studland.

I don't know exactly what went wrong. Perhaps the police put a stop to her activities as she had no licence. Or perhaps nobody wanted to buy warm Coca-Cola. Whatever the reason, I do know that she arrived home in a bad mood and with almost the same number of cans she had taken. She stacked the unopened crates of drinks in the garage, where they remained for years.

I once asked her if we could have one.

"Of course not," she said. "*Ach*, that would be drinking the profits."

Summer was drawing to a close, although Dorset was still packed with tourists. Hardly surprising as it is a particularly beautiful county with the most sunshine hours in England and more than its fair share of castles, stately homes, stunning coastline and ancient historical sites. My mother knew how attractive Dorset is to visitors, and predictably came up with another money-spinner.

"The giant!" she said one day at breakfast. "*Ja*, the giant with the massive erection."

My father coughed. We kids had no idea what she was talking about and carried on munching our toast, but my father stared at her. Then he hazarded a guess.

"Are you talking about the Cerne Abbas giant?"

The Cerne Abbas Giant

"Of course! I will take the kids to Chesil beach and we will collect suitable flat white stones. Then I will paint the Cerne Abbas giant on the stones and ask the tourist shops to sell them for me. They will sell like hot cakes! *Ach,* I can't understand why nobody has thought of it before!"

Near the village of Cerne Abbas is a particular hill. Centuries ago, the outline of a huge, well-endowed, naked man holding a knobbly club was carved out of the chalk hillside and can be seen for miles. Exactly how old the figure is, nobody is absolutely sure. It was mentioned in the 17th century but many historians believe it is much older; perhaps Medieval, or Roman, or Saxon, and some kind of fertility symbol.

The giant now belongs to the National Trust who maintain it. Renowned for his remarkable, eye-popping manhood, the Cerne Abbas giant is a huge tourist attraction. Hardly surprising that visitors flock to see it, as it must be Britain's most famous phallus. The giant's pride and joy measures some 11 metres (36 feet) high. Postcards of the giant in all his glory are the only 'indecent' photographs that can be sent through the English Post Office.

"Come on! We are going to collect stones," announced my mother.

We kids clambered into the back of Ivy and clung on as my mother crunched the gears and we set off.

"Chesil beach, here we come!" we shouted over the engine noise as Ivy bucked away, farting exhaust fumes along Dorset's country lanes.

Chesil beach has always fascinated me. It has been the scene of many a shipwreck and was a favourite port for smugglers, perhaps because of a unique feature. The shingle at the north-west end is pea-sized, but as one walks to the south-east end, the shingle gradually grows in size, until it is the size of oranges. It is said that smugglers who arrived in the dead of night without lights knew exactly where they were, just by the size of the shingle.

The beach is famous now, thanks to the 2007 novel, *On Chesil Beach,* but was also named by Thomas Hardy as 'Dead Man's Bay' because shipwrecks claimed so many lives.

We collected stones from the beach, and it turned out to be much less fun than we thought it would be. My mother was picky, and every stone we offered her had to pass the quality test.

"*Ach,* none of these stones are right!" she complained. "They are too round and lumpy, not flat enough. I do not think Chesil beach was the right place to come after all. Kids, we're going home."

As far as I can remember, we eventually found enough stones that were the right shape and size, and flat enough to paint on, not at Chesil, but at some other beach. Before long, the stones were washed and my mother painted a Cerne Abbas giant, with all his splendour on every one. The naked giants lay in long rows on our kitchen table, side by side, as my mother waited for them to dry. Next came a coat of varnish, and they were ready to sell.

Did my mother make a fortune selling her stones? I'm afraid not. I think she sold a few, but the remainder were returned to her by the tourist shops who were unable to sell them. She refused to dispose of them.

"What? Waste all that work?" she exclaimed.

So we shared our childhoods with these naked giants. They were used as paperweights, set into plant pots, lined up on windowsills, and given to anybody who visited the house.

The long summer days shortened and all too soon it was time to prepare for school again.

"*Ach,* your hair is far too long," said my mother peering at my brother.

My brother had spent the summer sticking together Airfix kits and model airplanes hung everywhere from his bedroom ceiling. When he had no more planes to assemble or paint, he devoted himself to dismantling things. My father had made him worktops which were crammed with stripped down toasters and radios. Whenever he put these things back together again, there always seemed to be bits left over.

"Sit on this stool, and I will cut your hair," said my mother.

My brother blinked at her, then perched obediently on a high kitchen stool and waited.

"*Ja,* this is what I need," she said, pulling a pudding basin from a cupboard and trying it on his head for size.

Out came the scissors and my brother's sun-bleached hair fell to the floor in clumps as she snipped around the edge of the bowl. Then she took off the bowl to admire her handiwork.

"Hmm... Perhaps some more off the top," she said, snipping thoughtfully.

"*Ach,* now the sides don't match..."

Snip-snip, went the scissors and my brother's hair dropped in clumps.

The result was no work of art. In fact, it looked as though my brother had been attacked by some particularly hungry caterpillars.

"*Ach,* it will do," she said and put the pudding basin and scissors away.

I wasn't looking forward to going back to school. Every day, my sister and I had to walk the mile and a half to Wareham station. The train steamed in, stopping at the platform with much puffing and blowing. We climbed aboard, bound for Dorchester. It seems strange now, but I don't ever remember being supervised. We just knew we mustn't stick our heads out of the window while the train was in motion or our heads would get chopped off.

On the first day back at school, Mrs Pellow, the headmistress, visited each classroom.

"Now children," she said, "do you remember what I asked you to do over the holidays?"

A forest of hands shot up into the air.

"Lucinda?"

"Miss, you said that we should write a composition about what we did in the holidays."

"Well done, Lucinda. That's right. And what did I say about these compositions?"

The forest of hands sprung up again.

"David?"

"Miss, you said the best one will win a prize."

I was sitting next to Nigel Harding. We looked at each other and pulled faces. I guessed he hadn't written a composition about what he did in the holidays either.

"Yes, David," said Mrs Pellow, "that's what I said, well done. But I have a wonderful surprise for you all. Not just the child who has written the best composition, but *everybody* who has written a composition is going to be given a *splendid* surprise!"

The class gasped. I gasped too, and so did Nigel Harding, but ours were gasps of horror. We hadn't written compositions so we'd get no splendid surprise.

One by one, our classmates handed over their compositions, and Mrs

Jam Roly-Poly

Serves 6

250g (8 oz) self-raising flour
Pinch of salt
50g (2 oz) light brown sugar
125g (4 oz) shredded suet
6 - 8 tbsp water
5 tbsp raspberry jam, warmed
Milk, for brushing
1 egg, beaten
Brown sugar, for glazing
Custard, for serving

Method
- Preheat the oven to 200C/400F/Gas Mark 6.
- In a bowl, add the brown sugar, flour and salt.
- Now add the suet and enough water to make a soft dough.
- Place the dough onto a floured surface and roll into a rectangle.
- Brush one side of the pastry with the warmed raspberry jam, leaving a 1cm (½ in) border.
- Fold the jamless border in and brush with milk.
- Loosely roll up the pastry, beginning with a short side of the rectangular pastry sheet.
- Seal the ends well.
- Place the pastry roll onto a greased baking sheet.
- Brush the pastry roll all over with the beaten egg and sprinkle with demerara sugar.
- Bake in the oven for 35-40 minutes, until cooked through.
- Remove from the oven and sprinkle on a little more brown sugar.
- Serve hot with custard.

Pellow gave each child a beaming smile and a splendid surprise. Nigel Harding's face was long, probably a reflection of mine.

"No composition?" asked Mrs Pellow as she reached us, her eyebrows raised in question.

"No, Miss."

"No, Miss."

"What a pity," said Mrs Pellow shaking her head sadly and passing by.

When our classmates opened their splendid surprises, our hearts were heavy. Each child was now the proud owner of a gyroscope. I pretended not to care, but I did.

A lot.

When I mentioned it at home, I got no sympathy. My big sister hardly looked up from playing with her gyroscope.

"*Ach*, you should have written your composition," said my mother.

I slouched off to see Timmy the tortoise.

I was too lazy, too much of a daydreamer and had my head stuck in a book too often to do well at school. The fact that my sister did so well academically made my lack of effort appear even worse. As far as I was concerned, if it wasn't reading, art, or animals, I wasn't interested.

❀ ❀ ❀

School Report
Reading: Victoria's reading is good for her age.
Writing: Victoria needs to be more careful.
Oral Composition: Rarely takes part, too busy daydreaming.
Written Composition: Good ideas but too slow getting them onto paper.
Arithmetic: Victoria struggles with this subject.
Nature Study: Keen.

❀ ❀ ❀

Leaves were beginning to redden and drift from the trees. Summer was truly over and our uniform changed from striped cotton dresses to long-sleeved white shirts, long grey socks and grey pinafore dresses.

My father made a box for Timmy to hibernate in. He filled it with straw and popped him in for the winter. Unfortunately, poor Timmy perished very early on. In those days, little was known about tortoise care, and the majority of pet tortoises died during their first hibernation. Happily, the import of tortoises into the UK for the pet trade is now illegal.

Of course I cried buckets of tears, and began to badger my mother for another pet. What I really wanted was a puppy I could take for walks on a lead, but I knew that would be out of the question.

"Please, *please* can I have a pet?"

My pleas were ignored.

"Why can't I have a guinea pig?"

"I told you, no more pets."

"What about a bird? A bird wouldn't be any trouble."

"*Ach,* you can have a bird but only if you catch one yourself."

She was joking, but I didn't know that. I clutched at the straw.

"Can I? Can I really? How do I catch one?"

"You have to put salt on its tail."

"Salt?"

"Yes, salt. That's how the rhyme goes:

> *He went to catch a dicky bird,*
> *And thought he could not fail,*
> *Because he'd got a little salt,*
> *To put upon his tail."*

"Salt? Is that how you catch a bird?"

"*Ach,* yes! Of course! Put some salt on his tail, and the bird will stand still. Then you can catch him and keep him as a pet."

I tried. I really tried. I stole salt from the larder and filled my pockets. I crept up behind birds as they landed on the lawn. But they always saw me coming and flew away with a whirr of wings before I had a chance to drop the salt on their tails.

"Does the salt work with any animals?" I asked.

"Oh, yes, just drop salt on their tails."

I began to plot.

Both my parents enjoyed sport. I'm told they first met at a tennis club. Later, we children were given tennis coaching as our parents felt that playing tennis would help us 'get on in life'. My mother was also a very good skier and used to ski a lot in her native Austria. My father could ski but his favourite sport was squash, and he was beginning to teach my sister the game.

I used to tag along, but *not* because I liked squash. On the contrary, I hated the smell of sweat at the courts, and the grunts that the players made, and the deafening thwack of the ball hitting the wall.

No, I had a hidden agenda. I had another reason for accompanying them to the squash courts.

5
Snowy and Snow

"Why do you want to come with us to squash?" asked my sister curiously. "Do you want to learn to play?"

"No, I'll just wait for you outside."

"Wouldn't you rather stay at home?" asked my father. "There's nothing to do there."

"That's okay, I'll play outside."

My father shook his head, baffled. I felt in my pocket. I had the salt cellar that I'd borrowed from the dining-room table, and a piece of string to use as a collar and leash. Now, which rabbit hole should I wait at?

The squash courts at Bovington Army Camp were surrounded by trees growing on banks. Dug into the banks and between the tree roots were numerous rabbit holes. I chose one and settled down to wait, the salt cellar poised ready to sprinkle on an unsuspecting bunny's tail.

I waited.

And waited.

Birds forgot I was there and settled quite close to me, scratching among the autumn leaves in search of something juicy for dinner. There were plenty of birds, but rabbits? I didn't see one.

In the distance I could hear the balls slamming against the squash court walls.

Thwack, thwack.

I still had time. I moved my cold, cramped legs and tried another rabbit hole.

Eventually the *thwacks* stopped and my father and sister emerged, hot and red-faced with exertion, to find me miserable and rabbitless.

"What on earth are you doing?" asked my father. "And why have you got your mother's best silver salt cellar?"

"I was trying to catch a rabbit to take home."

My sister rolled her eyes, but my father said nothing more as we drove home.

I imagine he felt sorry for me, because somehow he managed to persuade my mother that I could have a rabbit in the new year. It was decided that the space next to the proposed new workshop would be set aside for my rabbit.

Unfortunately, nothing happened until late the following spring. Although the old workshop was falling down, it couldn't be dismantled because a pair of robins were busily building their nest on a shelf.

I climbed on a stool and sneaked a peek at the nest. It looked very cosy, made from grass, leaves and lined with animal hair and moss.

I loved watching the mother sit on her little blue eggs. I watched her, and she watched me with her black beady eye.

"I'm pleased you are going to have a family," I told her, "but I wish you'd hurry up. I can't have my rabbit until your family is grown up."

One day, I visited the nest and there were four little orange gaping mouths in there. Mum and Dad were kept busy, arriving at regular intervals with beaks stuffed with caterpillars and other delicacies. My mother's passion for gardening meant they reaped the benefits of her vegetable garden and she frequently unearthed juicy worms for them.

"You are very cute," I told the baby birds, "but I wish you'd hurry up and grow and leave home."

At last the babies fledged, and the old workshop fell silent again. Now I had to wait for it to be pulled down and a new workshop to be erected. Adults were so slowwww.

While I waited, I had an idea. I would make myself a woodlouse sanctuary! I'd played with woodlice a lot, but I'd never tried keeping them as pets in my bedroom. I'd always liked woodlice and admired their ability to roll into shiny balls when alarmed. I had a nice shoebox with a tight-fitting lid; that would do perfectly! I decided not to tell the rest of the family about my plan as I was pretty sure they didn't share my fondness for woodlice. So I secretly went hunting in the garden and found plenty of the little creatures. I popped them into my box with old leaves, soil and included rotten wood for them to eat.

I'm not sure what I did wrong, but within a few days, every single woodlouse was dead. I still feel rather guilty about it.

"Why do you have a shoebox with earth and wood in it in your bedroom?" my mother asked.

"Oh, just something for art," I replied, relieved she hadn't noticed the corpses of my little pets.

The old workshop was pulled down, and a new one was built on the same site. My father constructed a hutch with compartments for both day and night, and the whole area was enclosed to make a run for the rabbit. My mother planted honeysuckle to make the area look more attractive.

I had saved my pocket money and visited the pet shop.

"Can I help you, love?" asked the lady behind the counter.

"I'd like a collar and lead, please," I said.

"What size would you like? What breed of dog?"

"Um, it's not exactly a dog."

"Oh, you'd like a ferret harness?"

"No, a collar and lead, please. For a rabbit."

"Sorry, speak up, love, did you say a rabbit?"

"Yes, please."

"Well, if you're sure… What colour would you like?"

"Red, please."

I ended up with a cat collar, complete with a bell, and a lead attached. I can't tell you how many times I drew that collar and lead out of the paper bag and admired them.

Everything was ready and I thought I might burst with excitement.

Our house with the new workshop

At last came the day when my father arrived home with a cardboard box. Something was scrabbling around in it, something with claws.

"*Ach*, open it," said my mother.

I lifted the flaps, and there, pressed into a corner was a white ball of fluff, a baby rabbit.

"Ohhhh…" I exhaled, already in love with the little thing.

I reached into the box and lifted her out, admiring her pink floppy ears and deep red eyes.

"What are you going to call her?"

"Twinkletoes."

"Not Snowy, like you said?"

"Well, her long name is Princess Snowy Twinkletoes the First."

"Well, take Princess Snowy Twinkletoes to her new enclosure, see if she likes it."

Princess Snowy did like it. She particularly liked the honeysuckle plants my mother had painstakingly planted. She didn't eat them, she just hopped along the row snipping them off at ground level with her razor teeth, ensuring they would never grow again. My mother was furious.

"I wouldn't mind so much if she ate them!" she fumed.

"She's just a baby," I said protectively. "She's probably teething."

But my mother never succeeded in growing honeysuckle around Princess Snowy's enclosure, and Snowy thrived. She grew bigger, and bigger.

Soon she was big enough to wear the collar and lead, and she came everywhere with me. It took a long time to go anywhere because she would hop this way and that, nibbling grass. People would stare at us, but I didn't care.

My rabbit was constantly hungry and soon grew to be a very large rabbit. And she developed a kick like a kangaroo. If she didn't want to be cuddled, which was all the time, a well-aimed kick in my stomach took all my breath away.

"I don't know why she's so unfriendly," I complained.

"*Ach*, perhaps she needs rabbit company," said my mother. "We'll take her over to the Hale's house today. I know the girls have a nice girl rabbit. Perhaps they'll be friends and it'll be nice for them both."

The Hale family lived on the opposite side of Wareham. To reach their huge, beautiful Tudor house, Ivy had to buck and fart her way through woods for quite some distance. Sometimes we glimpsed red squirrels as these woods were one of their last habitats before their bullying cousins, the grey squirrels, chased them off.

The house had been in the family for generations, and was breathtaking, with long oak-panelled corridors decorated with ancestral paintings. I wasn't much interested in the interior so I don't remember much about it, but I do remember being shown an ordinary-looking wardrobe in one of the bedrooms.

"Well, open it," Heather Hale said.

I did. It seemed normal enough to me. She leaned in and touched something, and the back wall slid sideways. I gaped at her.

"What is it?"

"A secret passage, of course," she said airily.

"Where does it go?"

"Not sure really."

"Have you ever been down it?"

"Nope. My brother and his friends did once, but it's all spidery and some of it's fallen in. Mummy says it's dangerous."

A secret passage! I was just discovering Enid Blyton and her *Famous Five* books, and *The Mystery of* series. I'd also read *The Lion, the Witch and the Wardobe*. I was in raptures.

Being Tudor, the house must have been built between 1485 and 1603, but I confess my knowledge of history is too poor to explain the purpose of the secret passage. If I was to hazard a guess, I'd say it was built for smugglers to hide their contraband, or escape from the law, as Dorset has a rich history of smuggling. Even more likely, it might have been a 'priest hole', a hiding place for priests, built into many English Catholic houses when Catholics were persecuted by law in England, from the beginning of the reign of Queen Elizabeth I in 1558.

But pirates, priest holes and secret passages were the last things on my mind that day. Princess Snowy Twinkletoes the First was on her leash and I led the way to the rabbit run where Heather's Miss Bunny sat on her hind legs daintily washing her face.

Princess Snowy suddenly saw Miss Bunny and stood stock still, staring, her nose twitching. She tensed, and made a beeline for Miss Bunny, bounding so fast that I had to run to keep up. The signs were good; it looked as though Princess Snowy was keen to play. Miss Bunny hopped to the front of her run and stood on her back legs, nose whiffling, front paws on the wire. Miss Bunny was much smaller than Snowy, but definitely interested in her new playmate. Princess Snowy was almost rigid with excitement as they touched noses through the wire mesh.

"Look!" I said, clasping my hands under my chin in delight. "Look how excited Snowy is, she can't wait to go in and play with Miss Bunny."

"I think they are going to be best friends," said Mrs Hale, smiling.

"*Ach,* put Snowy into the run and we can watch them play," said my mother.

Did we say *play?* Wrong word, wrong description. The instant that Princess Snowy's fluffy feet hit the ground, she was galloping after Miss

Bunny. Miss Bunny, a rather alarmed expression on her face, lolloped away from her pursuer. But Princess Snowy was on a mission and soon caught up. Miss Bunny froze as Snowy gripped her round the midriff, and pumped. My mouth dropped open.

"Oh!" said Mrs Hale.

"Golly!" said Heather.

"*Ach,*" said my mother.

"Oh look," I said, "Princess Snowy Twinkletoes and Miss Bunny are playing a lovely game together!"

"Hmm…" said my mother.

"Oh, look, they're playing that game *again!*" I said, as Miss Bunny broke free, chased by Snowy Twinkletoes.

"I think we may have misunderstood Princess Snowy Twinkletoes," said Mrs Hale grimly.

"*Ach,* I'm terribly sorry…" said my mother as Snowy climbed aboard Miss Bunny again. And again. And again.

Now there was no denying the fact that Snowy was a lusty buck rabbit, and not a female at all. And if we weren't willing to accept that, proof came 31 days later when Miss Bunny (now Mrs Bunny) gave birth to eleven kits. Snowy was confined to barracks, apart from walks on his leash, and allowed no more play dates.

The following winter took everybody by surprise. Many claim that Dorset is the warmest county in England as it is situated so far south and has more than its fair share of sunshine hours. However, even Dorset didn't escape the winter of 1962 -1963, soon to be called the Big Freeze.

Temperatures plummeted and were recorded as being the lowest since 1739. Astonishingly, lakes and rivers began to freeze over. Then on 26th December, Boxing Day, the snow arrived. The freezing temperatures and fierce winds created snowdrifts some 20 feet deep. Ordinary, maybe, for some parts of the world, but for England, freakish.

"*Ach,* I knew it was worth keeping my skis!" chortled my mother, and ordered my father to fetch them down from the attic.

Being Austrian, she was very much at home on skis, and I think she was secretly pleased not to drive Ivy for a while. She happily skied into Wareham to pick up bread and other necessities.

If late December was cold, January was even colder. The sea froze for a mile out from the shore at Herne Bay in Kent, and the upper reaches of the Thames began to freeze over, thick enough for people to skate on.

To me, Dorset became a fairytale setting of pristine, sparkling snow and silver icicles. Jack Frost painted his patterns on my bedroom window, and the world outside was blindingly white and silent.

Snowy Twinkletoes was moved into the garage for a while, but not before I'd set him down in the snow to see what he thought of it. Not much. He flicked the snow off his paws at every hop. I was surprised to see that he wasn't as white as I thought he was; against the virgin snow he looked quite yellow.

At the end of the Christmas holidays, school started again. Because of the weather, the trains had been cancelled, and a special bus was laid on. The bus set off valiantly but scarcely travelled a mile before it turned back, unable to negotiate the snowdrifts blocking the road. We were forced to stay at home and my happiness was complete.

That bitter winter dragged on for three long months. We went out very little, but that didn't bother me. I've always been happy in my own company, a dreamer. I was perfectly content in my room, weaving stories in my head, making things or reading. As my reading progressed, I developed an insatiable appetite for Enid Blyton, but I also remember a book called *A Tale of Two Horses*, and another, *Rascal the True Story of a Pet Raccoon*. I devoured whatever books I could lay my hands on, and never had enough.

But that was all about to change. New neighbours moved into the house two doors down from us. I was about to make lifelong friends.

6
Things That Go Bump

"Do our new neighbours have any children?" I asked.

"*Ach,* I believe they have one girl, two years younger than you."

I was walking past their house one day, and being curious, turned my head hoping for a glimpse of the new people. A lady was working in the front garden.

"Hello!" she said, straightening up from her task. "Aren't you Victoria from number 24?"

"Yes, I am," I answered shyly.

"Well, Victoria, I'm very pleased to meet you," she said, shaking my hand. "Come in and meet Annabel. She's making plaster of Paris models, perhaps you'd like to make some too?"

I followed her up the drive.

Plaster of Paris models? Now, that sounded like fun...

Annabel had curly hair and round, red cheeks and was even shyer than me. But after she'd explained the art of plaster of Paris modelling, and how one mixed the plaster into a paste and poured it into the rubber moulds, we were friends.

We set the models in rows to dry, then pulled off the moulds and hand-painted the features of the little hedgehogs and mice we'd made. Time flew past and we both forgot to be shy. Annabel's mother came in and admired our industry.

"I've just a baked a big chocolate cake, would you like to stay to tea?" she asked.

Chocolate cake? Would I! My mother rarely baked as she was far more interested in the plants in the garden. I couldn't believe my luck.

"Well, you'd better pop home and check that it's okay with your mother," said Annabel's mother. "And why don't you call me Auntie Jean?"

I did pop home and was back in a trice. We sat down at the big table in the kitchen; Annabel, Auntie Jean, Uncle Frank and me. The chocolate cake was delicious and we drank cups of tea out of china teacups and saucers decorated with flowers. I was in heaven. This was the first of many, many teas I would be invited to over the years. As Annabel and I grew up, her house became as important to me as my own.

Annabel's house was huge, bigger than ours, and the garden was wonderful. The lawn was so big that Uncle Frank would sit on his mower to cut the grass, but the shrubs provided Annabel and me with dens to hide in and read comics like *June and School Friend, Bunty* and *Mandy.* Often Tibby, their grey and white cat, would join us, stretching out luxuriously to have his tummy rubbed or his chin scratched.

The garden had a huge buddleia bush that attracted hundreds of butterflies all summer long. Annabel and I caught them in butterfly nets and trapped them in the sun parlour, only to let them go again, watching them float out of the windows, back to the blue flowers of the buddleia bush.

Annabel's house had so many attractions. There were unused rooms to play in, and places to explore. There were huge polished tables, perfect for making dens beneath when the weather was bad. Auntie Jean never interfered, and never scolded us for making a mess, instead bringing us trays of cookies and milk to eat in our dens. I adored her.

I believe it was at Annabel's house that I saw my first television set. It was big and ugly, and the pictures were in black and white, of course. I remember dreadful shows like *The Black and White Minstrel Show* and *Sunday Night at the London Palladium.* For years, my parents refused to have a television in their house, probably rightly so, considering the nonsense that was being aired.

And the books in Annabel's house! Shelves and shelves of

Auntie Jean and Tibby

Enid Blyton books like *The Faraway Tree, The Naughtiest Girl* series, *The Secret Seven, Famous Five,* all of them!

As I grew older, my insatiable appetite for reading was satisfied by Auntie Jean's pile of *Good Housekeeping* magazines, and the adult books I found, like the *Readers' Digests.* Once I found a book called *Lady Chatterley's Lover* by D. H. Lawrence. Intrigued, I took it home without asking, and read it under my bedcovers, my eyes round with disbelief. I didn't understand a word of it, but I knew it was very, very rude. I didn't know that the book had been banned and was only released in 1960 following a sensational trial.

But best of all, I loved the boarding school stories like *Malory Towers*. Boarding school life sounded such fun, I thought, little knowing that I would soon experience it for myself.

In those days, we didn't use the term 'sleepover' but Annabel and I had many. I loved staying the night, and, fired up by our reading of *Malory Towers*, we planned midnight feasts.

"What shall we eat?" asked Annabel.

"Let's raid the pantry."

It was silly really. Auntie Jean would have given us anything we asked for, but it was more fun to secretly make a stash. We found chocolate cookies, cake and a packet of meringue nests. That would do nicely. We hid our stash in the cupboard under the stairs, went to bed giggling, and set the alarm clock for midnight, hiding it under a pillow to muffle it.

The next morning, we woke as Auntie Jean drew the heavy curtains to allow the new day in.

"Did you have a nice night?" she asked. "Sleep well?"

Annabel and I sat up and rubbed our eyes, then looked at each other. Was it morning? Had we forgotten to wake up? Had we missed our own midnight feast? Apparently we had.

Luckily, I was staying another night, so we tried again. We set the clock, determined not to sleep through it this time.

At the stroke of midnight the alarm shrilled, and we both woke up. It was tempting to just turn it off and go back to sleep, but that's not what the girls at Malory Towers would have done. Neither of us felt the slightest bit hungry, but we tumbled out of bed nevertheless.

"Ssshhh... Watch the third step down, it's a creaky floorboard," whispered Annabel.

Creak!

Too late, I'd already stood on it.

We froze, praying that Auntie Jean and Uncle Frank hadn't woken up. Nothing stirred. Sighing with relief, we tiptoed down the remainder of the stairs, opened the cupboard door, slipped in, and turned on the light.

Two little girls in a cramped under-stairs cupboard, giggling, scoffing chocolate cookies, and shushing each other, are bound to make a lot of noise. We had no idea what was happening upstairs.

"Frank? Frank! There's somebody downstairs!"

"What?"

"I think we've got burglars!"

"Burglars?"

"Yes! I can hear strange noises!"

"What sort of noises?"

"Well, listen!"

Now they were both sitting up in bed.

"I can hear giggling!"

"It's the girls. Whatever are they doing? I'm going to look."

Auntie Jean tiptoed to the top of the stairs and looked down before returning to the bedroom.

"They're in the cupboard under the stairs," she whispered. "I can see the light through the cracks. I think they're having a midnight feast."

"Burglars indeed! Don't you go disturbing them. Let them get on with it, they'll soon come back to bed."

That's the way they were. Annabel and I finished our midnight feast and tiptoed back to bed, totally unaware that Jean and Frank knew all about it.

❋ ❋ ❋

My sister, being four years older than I, had already left Mrs Pellow's Preparatory School and moved on to another school called Talbot Heath. Now it was my turn.

My sister had sailed through the Common Entrance exam, the test that is needed to be passed before Talbot Heath would accept a pupil. I was 11 years old and needed to take the Common Entrance as well as the 11+ exam along with it.

The 11+ exam is so called because it was taken by children aged 11 or older. Passing the 11+ meant one could go to a Grammar School, a school for pupils with academic ability. Failing it meant one attended a Secondary Modern school to learn vocational skills such as cooking, typing or car maintenance. This was before the days of the Comprehensive school system. Both the Common Entrance and 11+ exams were administered at Mrs Pellow's Preparatory School.

It didn't help that I was often off school, suffering from frequent sore throats and a stuffy nose.

"Hmm…" said our family doctor. "It might be a good idea if we arrange to have Victoria's adenoids removed."

Exam day arrived. Instead of our usual teacher, Mrs Pellow herself was going to supervise us. The desks were arranged in straight rows, and we filed in alphabetically. I was terrified.

"Now, children," said Mrs Pellow, "you must do your best. I know you are all very nervous, so I've brought you something to buck you up."

Now we were interested. Mrs Pellow paced up and down the lines of desks.

"Mrs Pellow's Pep Pills for Pallid Pupils," she said, plonking a tube of Smarties in front of every child.

Suddenly the exams didn't feel so bad.

"Eat some and then rub the back of your necks to get the sugar to the brain."

Really? Okay!

"When I tell you, turn over the paper and write today's date in the box provided. Do it now!"

With a rustle of paper, we did as instructed.

"Now write your date of birth in the box below it."

We obeyed as Mrs Pellow prowled up and down the line of desks checking that we were doing it correctly. At my desk, she stopped. A large finger stabbed at the two boxes I'd just filled in.

"You've written the same date twice," she said, and my heart raced.

"Yes, Miss."

In the first box I'd written today's date: *17th February 1966*. In the box below I'd written my date of birth: *17th February 1955*.

"It's my birthday today," I whispered.

"Good gracious!" she bellowed. "Then you must have *another* tube of Mrs Pellow's Pep Pills for Pallid Pupils!"

Sadly, despite the double dose of medication, I didn't pass the Common Entrance exam, although I did pass the 11+. Graciously, Talbot Heath School for Girls, or TH as we soon called it, accepted me anyway. They reasoned that because my sister was so smart, it must have been a fluke that I failed their entrance exam. Little did they know that my sister was far more academically gifted and motivated than I would ever be.

As with every final year in Primary School, our class was planning to put on a big show for the parents. Ours was going to be a musical, poetry and dance extravaganza, staged at Dorchester Corn Exchange. My poem was part of *The Walrus and the Carpenter* from Lewis Carroll's *Through the Looking Glass* and I knew it by heart. I could recite it with ease in my bedroom and in the bath, and can still remember much of it today.

> *"The time has come," the Walrus said,*
> *"To talk of many things:*
> *Of shoes - and ships - and sealing-wax -*
> *Of cabbages - and kings -*
> *And why the sea is boiling hot -*
> *And whether pigs have wings."*

A wonderful poem, full of humour and irony, and every word was burned into my brain. The problem was my shyness. As soon as I opened my mouth to recite anything in front of anybody, except Snowy Twinkletoes and Annabel, my mind went blank. My mouth opened, but nothing came out.

"Victoria, you *know* this poem," said my exasperated teacher, Miss Gunson. "You need to be able to recite it next week at the Corn Exchange, word perfect. Now come on, try!"

I did try, but the words remained locked away and hidden. Of course, as soon as Miss Gunson passed to another child, the words came flooding back.

And if that wasn't bad enough, I was also taking part in the dance routine. It began with a country dance liberally sprinkled with 'dozy-does' and 'under the arches'.

For the dance, the boys would be wearing blue checked shirts, and the girls would wear blue checked dresses with petticoats. I loved my costume. I also loved the dance, but I struggled. I must have been Miss Gunson's worst nightmare.

"Victoria, peel off to the *left*, not right! Good. Now under the arch… No, *under* it, not round it… Take your partner, spin to the right… *Right,* not left! Now, skip-skip-skip… Victoria, apologise to Nigel, I think you skipped quite heavily on his toe..."

I practised in my bedroom at home, determined to get it right before the big performance. Spin to the right, skip-skip-skip...

"*Ach!* Victoria! What are you doing up there? You sound as if you are coming through the ceiling!"

Before the day of the Extravaganza, I heard our telephone ring.

"Wareham 297," said my mother. In those days, all telephones were heavy, black, dial affairs, and telephone numbers were just three digits.

"Yes, I'm sure that would be possible. Yes, we'll bring her then. Thank you for admitting her. Goodbye." She replaced the receiver with a clatter.

"Victoria, that was Poole General Hospital. It seems they have an unexpected vacancy and they want to take you in next week to remove your adenoids. That's good, isn't it?"

"But what about the Extravaganza?"

"*Ach,* I'm afraid you'll have to miss it."

"But I'm reciting my poem! And what about the Rustic Dance? Nigel won't have a partner, and I can't wear my costume…" My bottom lip was a-tremble.

"I'm afraid the hospital won't wait. You'll have other chances to perform when you go to Talbot Heath."

So that was that. I never did perform at the Corn Exchange, and Miss

Gunson probably celebrated when she heard I wouldn't be there. I'm sure the performance went without a hitch.

Now I had something new to worry about; the removal of my adenoids.

7
TH

I didn't even know what adenoids were, but it seemed that I was scheduled for a stay in hospital to have mine removed. From the 1930s through to the 1960s, tonsillectomies and adenoidectomies were routine operations and thousands were performed every year. Nowadays, doctors are more enlightened and know that most of those operations were unnecessary and probably unwise. But, when I was a child, they were extremely common procedures.

"My brother had that," said Nigel Harding enviously. "He was allowed to eat as much ice cream as he wanted for three days!"

Suddenly the prospect of the operation didn't seem quite so daunting. I was admitted to the hospital and my parents drove away. Parents were not allowed to stick around in those days.

The hospital was built in 1907, and was largely demolished in the 1960s to make way for a new hospital of 500 beds. However, the Children's Ward was still housed in an old wing. The ceilings were high and the floors were bare. Even the slightest noise echoed.

Sure enough, after my operation, the nurses offered me ice cream. I had ice cream every day, sometimes with jelly. On the third day I was feeling much better and becoming accustomed to the hospital routine. In the evening, the radio and all the lights were switched off, and a night nurse sat working at a desk in the centre of the ward, a single lamp illuminating her. The ward was silent. The night nurse occasionally stood, yawned, and walked round the beds, shining a torch on each sleeping child in turn.

"Aren't you asleep yet?" she whispered when she reached me.

I shook my head.

"Not yet," I whispered back.

Suddenly, a female scream ripped through the night.

"Aaaaaaagh!"

The night nurse and I froze in shock, our mouths agape. What was happening? The scream wasn't coming from our ward, but from somewhere along the corridor, and it was getting closer.

"Aaaaaaagh!"

The night nurse's hand tightened on her torch. She trembled as she turned on her heel and trained the beam on the closed ward door, just as it burst open.

"Aaaaaaagh!" screamed a nurse as she ran into the ward towards us. "Bats! BATS! The place is alive with bats!"

The night nurse dropped her torch and jumped into my bed, pulling the blanket over her head. The screaming nurse ran for the door again, slamming it shut behind her.

I stood by my bed and looked up. Two or three bats were flitting high up in the rafters. They didn't scare me at all.

A muffled voice emerged from the depths of my bed.

"Have they gone?"

"The other nurse has gone," I said. "But the bats are still here. They are very high up. They won't hurt you, you know."

The night nurse's face peeped out from under my bedclothes, her face as white as my sheets.

"You stay here," she said at last. "I'm going to get help."

With as much dignity as she could muster with a hospital blanket over her head, the nurse strode to the door and let herself out. I was alone with the bats and a ward full of sleeping children.

A caretaker came in next, armed with a big net. I watched, fascinated, as he attempted to catch the bats. He failed, but successfully shooed the little creatures out of the ward and into the corridor. The night nurse returned, smoothing down her apron and pushing escaped tendrils of hair back into her cap.

"Still not asleep?" she whispered. "Let me sort your bed out for you."

She replaced my blanket and I snuggled down, tired now. None of the other children had wakened. I closed my eyes and slept. My dreams were filled with bats and country dancing.

I learned later that a colony of bats had inhabited the old hospital. They had been disturbed by the ongoing demolition works, and some had entered the hospital, visiting several wards, including ours. I hoped that they moved on without too much trauma and found a safe new home.

It was also time for me to move on. I never saw Mrs Pellow, Nigel Harding or Dorchester Preparatory School again. I would now move on to Talbot Heath (TH), following in my big sister's footsteps. I only hoped that Enid Blyton had been telling the truth about boarding school life.

❋ ❋ ❋

School Report
Reading: Victoria reads well although shyness holds her back.
Writing: Careless, although she has a good command of words.
Written Composition: Victoria enjoys this and has made progress.
Mathematics: Has the impression that this subject is too difficult for her.

What a pity Victoria wastes so much time because she has ample ability. She has given up with mathematics which is silly and pointless. She must do the Arithmetic and English Progress Papers I have given her during the holidays. Please ensure she does them daily, not in a rush just before the TH term starts!

Joan Pellow (headteacher)

❀ ❀ ❀

Before school term started, there was a lot to do. Apart from the awful Progress Papers that I had to wrestle with every day, there was packing. My father heaved a huge trunk into my bedroom. There it remained, like a giant open coffin, slowly filling up in readiness for the new term. TH had provided us with an inventory, and every tiny thing on that list had to be checked off, right down to colour of shoe polish. Astonishingly, the particular brown required was called by a word that was soon to be banned, a word that rhymes with 'bigger'. We had no idea the word was so insulting or controversial. Of course this particular shade has been renamed now.

There were the summer and uniforms. In winter we wore navy blue pinafore dresses with white blouses underneath. We had to wear stockings and suspenders because tights hadn't been invented yet. The stockings were usually a disgusting shade called 'American Tan' and had to be 60-90 denier, making them virtually bullet-proof. We also had to wear gloves and navy blue felt hats. In summer, we wore gingham dresses and white socks with blazers and straw boaters.

Then there was *mufti*, or non-uniform clothes. We were allowed a couple of summer dresses, a pair of trousers, a pair of shorts, and some tops.

Sports equipment, such as hockey sticks and tennis racquets, needed to be packed. Black swimming costumes, and culottes (short trousers that looked like skirts) were included. We also needed bed sheets, towels, dressing gown, slippers and wash stuff.

Then there were some puzzling items that needed explaining, like the *6 pairs of white cotton linings*. And *3 pairs of navies with pocket*.

"*Ach,*" said my mother, already familiar with this requirement because of my sister's packing in previous years. "Linings just means underpants. And navies are navy blue knickers to go over the top."

"What's the pocket for?"

"I don't know. A hanky maybe?"

Every pupil also needed to bring a sanitary belt and two packs of Dr White's sanitary towels. These were enormous pads with loops either end, not like the neat, flat, self-adhesive pads that are available nowadays.

"What are these?" asked my brother, waving one at me.

He was preparing to go to boarding school too, and Dr White's were certainly not on his list of requirements.

"Oh, they're in case you get a nosebleed," I said. "You hook those loops over your ears."

He seemed satisfied with that, and left me to carry on packing.

Every item had to be labelled with our name and laundry number (mine was SY16) if it was to be sent to the laundry. My mother never claimed to be a domestic goddess, and sewing on those endless Cash's name-tapes must have driven her crazy.

I was to be in St Mary's, one of three houses set in pine woodlands some distance from the school. St Mary's was three floors high and had long stone-floored corridors. The ground floor was given over to the kitchen, dining room, Matron's office, prefects' rooms and two common rooms: one for the seniors and the other for juniors. Upstairs were the dormitories (or dorms), bathrooms and the Housemistress's suite.

St Mary's today

The dormitories already felt quite familiar to me as I had previously visited them with my sister. There were eight high metal beds, each with a metal locker beside it. No curtains, no privacy, but it never occurred to me at that age that I needed it.

On that first day, I was the last to arrive. The dorm was buzzing with noise and chaotic with half-unpacked trunks. Parents milled around, helping their daughters settle in. My father was in the doorway, dragging my trunk inside. Overcome with shyness, I looked around. Every bed seemed to be taken.

"*Ach*, I can't see a spare bed," said my mother.

A girl with straight blonde hair looked up from the locker she was filling. She and I stared at each other for a moment. There was a naughty glint in her eye which I liked immediately.

"This bed next to me is empty," she said, and her smile lit up her face.

I found myself smiling back at her, and in that moment I knew I had a friend.

Soon, the parents had to leave but I scarcely noticed mine go. Helen and I had finished our unpacking and were sitting side by side on her bed, swinging our legs and chattering about whatever eleven-year-olds chatter about.

Our dorm was on the first floor, and below it was the junior common room. The common room was fitted out with mismatching tables and chairs and some threadbare comfy chairs. We had an old-fashioned record player with a needle that scratched our records if we jogged it, but only a few records. The strains of *Homeward Bound* by Simon and Garfunkel even now immediately transports me back to the common room. That and the taste of butterscotch sweets, which were my tuck item of choice. After lunch every day, Matron unlocked the tuck cupboard and we were permitted just two of the sweets we had stashed.

I fitted into boarding school life fairly happily. I didn't see much of my sister as she was already in the upper school and used a different common room. But I made friends quite easily, especially after my housemates realised that my initial silence was due to shyness. As soon as I felt comfortable, I was as lively as the others. In fact, I was usually in more trouble than most, except perhaps for my best friend Helen.

To exit the building, one had to walk along a lengthy corridor, past the locker room where we kept our coats and outside shoes, and out of the back door. It was just my luck that I bumped into Matron just after I'd taken a shortcut.

"Victoria! Did I just see you jumping out of the common room window?"

"Yes, Matron."

"Good heavens! You know we can't allow our gels to jump out of windows! Whatever next?" Matron tried hard to sound cultured, and girls were always 'gels'.

"It's not very high."

"Nevertheless, I shall require you to write me two hundred lines, *I must not jump out of the window.*"

My heart sank.

"Yes, Matron."

"By chapel this evening."

"Yes, Matron."

As if our nightly visits to chapel weren't bad enough, now I had to waste time writing lines as well. I enlisted the help of Helen and some other friends, and luckily Matron never noticed the sudden changes of handwriting styles. This was common practice, and I learned always to offer help with other people's lines, in readiness for when I was given my own to complete.

Matron was a formidable lady. She wore a white starched uniform and white cap perched squarely on her red hair which was rolled up into some sort of pleat. The white lace-up shoes she wore were utterly silent, allowing her to prowl around without a sound. Her footsteps may have been silent, but Matron's booming voice could be heard from the other side of the building.

"Gels! Gels! You are not permitted into the dining room except at meal times!"

With a rustle of uniform, she bore down on us.

"Gels! Out you go, unless you want to write some lines for me?"

No, we didn't. We exited swiftly.

Matron had her favourites, and I wasn't one of them. You knew if Matron liked you because on Sunday evenings, which were hair-wash days, Matron let a small group of girls into her room to dry their hair in front of the two-bar electric fire she had there. I don't think any of us had heard of hair dryers then, and we certainly didn't own one. Matron's door would close and we'd hear the sound of laughter as her favourites dried their hair and helped themselves to Matron's tin of Scottish shortbread.

Of course, anybody who courted trouble, as I and my friend Helen did, would never get to dry her hair in Matron's room.

It was Matron who ran St Mary's House, but it was Mrs Driver who was officially in charge. Mrs Driver, the Housemistress, was a mannish, secretive person who spent most of her time in her suite of rooms on the top floor. She had grey hair that she scraped back from her face and stuck down flat to her skull with water, or perhaps Brylcreem. Half-moon glasses hung from a chain around her neck, bouncing on her ample bosom as she walked.

Mrs Driver owned a pop-eyed Chihuahua called Brandy. Twice a day, Mrs Driver and Brandy would emerge from their rooms and descend the stairs. Mrs Driver smelled the same as the Roman Catholic priest from whom we bought our house in Wareham. Her eyes were glazed over, and she looked at nobody, neither did she speak as she walked down the steps.

On the other hand, Brandy, the Chihuahua, had something important on his mind. As Mrs Driver continued down the stairs, Brandy searched in vain for a mate. He charged into our dorm, and finding no lady dog to cool his ardour, was forced instead to make do with a slipper, or teddy, or pile of clothes on the floor.

"Brandy!" called Mrs Driver from the bottom of the stairs, and away he scampered to join his mistress.

"She should have called that bloody dog Randy," I once heard Matron mutter after Brandy had assaulted an unsuspecting wastepaper basket in her office.

"Pardon, Matron?"

"Nothing. Helen, Victoria, haven't you gels got anything to do? Run along and do some schoolwork or something."

Boarding school culture was fascinating. For a start, there was a whole new language to learn. Luckily I didn't have a problem with that, as my big sister had already taught me many of the words. For instance, a wastepaper basket was a 'wagger', and a petticoat was a 'charlie'. If a girl's petticoat happened to show beneath the hemline of her skirt, one had to sidle up to her and quietly hiss, "Charlie's dead!" thus alerting her to the petticoat calamity.

Nobody was called by her real name. We didn't resort to surnames, as happened in most boys' boarding schools, but each girl was given a nickname. My best friend Helen was called Snort because of the one time she snorted in her sleep. I was named Dusty because somebody said my eyes were as big as dustbin lids.

There were other strange rituals that had become traditional at TH. For example, the mysterious Nelson's Eye which filled us youngsters with fear.

Summer Pudding

Serves 4

1 large, white organic loaf, thickly sliced, crusts removed
Approximately 1.5 kg (3 lbs) of mixed red soft fruit, whichever
summer berries are in season, the juicier the better eg: raspberries,
cherries, blueberries, strawberries, boysenberries, blackberries,
redcurrants, blackcurrants, etc.
1 cup of sugar
Zest of 1 lemon
Clotted, whipped or pouring cream (optional)

Method
- Wash the fruit and remove any stones, pips, stalks, etc.
- Butter the inside of a 1.5 litre (3 pint) pudding basin.
- Line the pudding basin with the bread slices, slightly overlapping each slice so there are no gaps between, and pressing the edges together so the bread forms a complete shell inside the bowl.
- Bring the mixed berries, lemon zest and sugar to a gentle simmer, for about 5 minutes, until the sugar is dissolved and the fruits are releasing their juice. Allow the fruit to keep its shape. Take care not to overcook.
- Reserve about ¾ cup of juice and put it to one side to cool, then refrigerate.
- Pour the rest of the fruit and juice into the bread-lined pudding basin.
- Seal the top completely with further, overlapping, slices of bread.
- Cover the bread with a small flat plate or saucer that fits snugly inside the basin.
- Weigh down the plate with weights or a very heavy can or jar.
- Leave in the fridge overnight. The weight will cause the juice to bleed through the bread staining it red.
- Before serving, gently slide a flexible spatula between the bread and the basin to loosen.
- Invert the bowl onto a serving plate, the pudding should slide easily into place.
- Use the reserved juice to colour any areas that still have a white tinge. Pour any remaining juice over the top of the pudding.
- Serve with a dollop of cream.

8
Day by Day

"We've been here a week," said Snort, "and they haven't made us do Nelson's Eye yet."

"I know," I said, shivering. "It'll probably be this weekend. I'm dreading it."

The week had been packed with activities and we had begun to learn the routine we would follow for the next few years. It's possible that I haven't remembered the times correctly, or have left out huge gaps, but this is roughly how I remember a typical day's routine.

6.55 Wake-up bell.

A bell to be ignored.

7.00 Get-out-of-bed bell.

"Gels! Up you get!" called Matron. "Come on, you gels, hurry up, get washed. Victoria, make sure you tidy the top of your locker, it's a disgrace."

Out she rustled, making her way to the next dorm to continue spreading her cheer.

Snort and I dragged ourselves out of bed, grabbed our towels and wash things and trudged towards the bathroom. There were no showers, just cubicles with a washbasin in each. There were two baths, in separate cubicles, but we were only allowed a bath once a week. The bathrooms were unheated and every sound echoed. We splashed water on our faces and cleaned our teeth.

"You ready, Snort?"

"Yup."

Back in the dorm, we pulled on our uniforms and knee-high socks, and buckled our Clarke's sandals. On our first morning, Matron had ordered the whole dorm to kneel down in front of her.

"Gels, I am checking your hemlines. No skirt should be more than two inches off the ground when you kneel down. Cindy, kneel up straight, it's no good slouching, I'll still know if your skirt is too short."

"But Matron, I've got big knees..."

Reluctantly, Corkscrew (as we called Cindy on account of her curly hair) straightened up. Along came Matron with her ruler, measuring the distance between hemline and floor. Snort passed, and I, too, passed easily as my mother belonged to the buy-it-much-too-big-she'll-grow-into-it-eventually school of thought. My hemline was probably a good two inches *below* the knee, not above.

Corkscrew's hemline failed, being a racy three and a half inches above the knee. Corky was told to wear her PE culottes and her mother was summoned and ordered to buy a new dress.

There was still another job to do before breakfast.

"Don't forget to strip your beds, gels!" Matron called.

Even now, I'm usually one of those sleepers who barely disturbs the bed. I'm not the type who kicks off the bedclothes or tosses and turns during the night. So I deeply resented the fact that we had to completely strip our beds every morning. Just pulling the covers back to let the bed air should be enough, surely?

7.30 Breakfast bell.

Now it was time to line up outside the dining hall, juniors on one side, seniors on the other. As we filed in, Matron dished out an orange tablet to each girl, a multi-vitamin, cod liver oil concoction called Haliborange. My mother thought vitamin supplements were a waste of time and money, so I was not given one. I rarely suffer from colds or ill health now *(touch wood)*, so I wonder whether perhaps she was right.

Mrs Driver and Matron sat at a separate table, and we girls were seated in long rows. Brandy the Chihuahua roamed the dining hall, looking for feet to hump. Then Mrs Driver or one of the prefects would say Grace, always the same words:

For what we are about to receive, may the Lord make us truly thankful.
Amen.

Once, when my sister became a prefect and it was her turn to say Grace at the midday meal, I couldn't believe my ears. We all put our hands together and bowed our heads, waiting for her to speak.

"God bless this bunch as they munch their lunch," she said.

The dining hall gasped. Snort and I exchanged glances, waiting for the fallout. Mrs Driver and Matron flicked glances at her, but said nothing.

Breakfast consisted of cornflakes, eggs and toast. On Fridays there was steamed fish that made my stomach heave. In the winter, we queued into the kitchen to receive a dollop of porridge, which I loved.

By eight o'clock, we were well into our breakfast. Mrs Driver twiddled with the knob of the huge radio on the shelf above her. First it crackled, the signal for us to fall silent. Then, exactly on the hour, came the pips.

This is the BBC World Service. Here is the news.

Whatever the prime minister, Harold Wilson, said in parliament, or the fact that the village of Milton Keynes was to be developed and declared a 'New Town' passed over my head. Snort and I were more interested to hear that police raided the home of Rolling Stones musician Keith Richards, following a tip-off from the *News of the World*, and charged him and Mick Jagger with the possession of drugs.

After breakfast, we raced up the stairs back to the dorm. I'd tried to disguise the fact that I hadn't stripped my bed but somebody had been in while we'd been at breakfast and stripped it completely. We then set about remaking our beds.

If it was a Thursday, we had to take off the bottom sheet and replace it with the top. Then we'd collect a clean sheet from the laundry cupboard. Snort and I helped each other making our beds, both hoping that there was a diamond shape in the centre of the clean sheet when we unfolded it. If there was, that meant good luck for the week.

We made our beds with hospital corners, which would be checked by Matron. Then we tidied our lockers, ran downstairs to sort out our school satchels and were then ready to slip through the woods, past the Biology pond, (known as the Bug Pond) to the school building.

Lessons dragged on, one after the other. The highlight was break-time when all the boarders were given a fresh bun from the bakery. Sometimes it was a Chelsea bun dotted with currants, or an iced bun, or jam doughnut. The day girls (we called them Day Bugs) clustered around the boarders.

"Let's have a taste!" they begged.

Sometimes I felt very lucky to be a boarder, not a Day Bug.

Each girl belonged to a 'house', like the houses in Harry Potter's school, Hogwarts: Gryffindor, Slytherin, Ravenclaw, and Hufflepuff. TH had 12 houses, each named after a famous person. I was put in my sister's house, Elizabeth Fry, as siblings always belonged to the same house. We wore dark green enamel badges edged with gold to show which house we belonged to. My friend Snort was in Shackleton, and her badge was a much nicer shade of blue. The aim of the house system was to foster group loyalty and encourage competition with each other at sports and academic subjects, thus perhaps achieving more. Unfortunately, I have never had a competitive spirit, and the house system didn't encourage me to perform better at all.

When school ended, the Day Bugs went home and we boarders carried our satchels back through the woods to St Mary's.

"Every time we walk through the woods, I think of Nelson's Eye," said Snort unhappily.

"Me too. I hope they don't do it this year."

We ran upstairs to our dorm and changed out of our uniforms and into mufti.

Next was teatime in the dining hall. This was a more relaxed meal, as we didn't need to queue, or say Grace. We could come and go as we pleased and sit wherever we liked. Mounds of sliced white bread awaited us on the tables, and plastic tubs of almost white, unappetising, margarine. There was always jam, sometimes boiled eggs, and some kind of cake, plus big urns full of tea. On some days, the kitchen staff beat Marmite into the margarine, and the resulting grey stuff was heaped into a bowl. We called it Marmite Squish. Snort loved it and I hated it.

16.00 Prep bell.

If Snort and I wolfed down our tea quickly, there would be some spare minutes when we could just loaf about before Prep. Prep took place in the common room from 4 o'clock until 5, and was the time when we were supposed to do our homework. Talking was not permitted. Sometimes Matron supervised Prep, or one of the prefects. Snort and I rushed through our homework then spent the remainder of the time writing notes to each other.

"Are you two gels passing notes to each other? Helen, Victoria?"

"Yes, Matron."

"Then you must each write one hundred lines. *I must not write notes in Prep.*"

"Yes, Matron."

Long faces.

Next came a spare hour when we could do what we liked. We weren't allowed to keep pets, but in springtime, Snort and I pulled out some frogspawn from the Bug Pond and put it in jars on the windowsill in the cloakroom. As the tadpoles transformed into tiny froglets, we used old toothbrushes to brush greenfly from the roses growing in the flowerbeds. These we fed to our froglets.

Sometimes Mrs Driver would pass by, with Brandy close behind.

"What are you two doing?" she asked once.

"Getting food for our froglets, Miss," said Snort.

Mrs Driver raised her eyebrows, but didn't enquire further. Giving her head a shake, she called Brandy who quit humping the cardigan Snort had dropped on the lawn and trotted after his mistress.

18.00 Chapel bell.

We went to chapel every evening, even on Sundays when we also went to church. Chapel was dull, and being a dreamer, I just disappeared into my own head. Snort was a wriggler, so was often in trouble.

Dinner followed, then a little more free time, then bed. Lights-out was at 8.30, and woe betide if you were caught talking after that.

"Pssst! Dusty? Are you asleep?"

"Nope," I replied.

"I was thinking about Nelson's Eye," said Snort.

"What about it?"

"Couldn't you ask your sister about it? She could tell us if they are still going to do it."

"I already did."

"What did she say?"

"She said it was strictly forbidden for anybody to talk about Nelson's Eye."

"Oh. Can't she break the rule? We wouldn't tell."

"No. She says if anybody breaks the rule, the ghost of Emily the scullery maid will haunt them until the day they leave TH."

"Oh."

"Ssssh, you two!" hissed a voice from another bed. "Some of us are trying to get to sleep here!"

"Sorry!"

"Sorry!"

Pause.

"Snort?"

"What?"

"I don't really believe in the ghost of Emily the scullery maid, do you?"

The dorm door opened, throwing a triangle of light into the dorm.

"Helen! Victoria! I could hear you gels from outside the door. You will both write me one hundred lines tomorrow, *I must not talk after lights-out.*"

Sigh.

"Yes, Matron."

"Yes, Matron."

Weekends panned out differently, of course, because there was no school. Every third weekend or so was an 'exeat' which meant our parents could take us out for the day. Usually, my father arrived in our black Rover 90, but I much preferred it when Ivy came to collect us. The day was fun but rather curtailed because we had to go to church first, and be back in time for evening chapel.

Church was obligatory on Sunday, as was chapel every evening. Snort and I always sat together in chapel and walked together to church. We were dressed in our best uniform, with stockings, white gloves, and hats. The whole of St Mary's walked in a crocodile of girls to one of two churches, headed by Mrs Driver with Matron bringing up the rear. For once, the amorous Brandy was left at home which was probably just as well considering how many kneelers the Women's Institute had embroidered, all of which he would have assaulted.

Sometimes we walked through the Bournemouth public gardens and across a golf course. The walk was nice, but the destination was dull. As the sermon ate into our precious free time, Snort and I yearned to be outside.

Because Snort was a wriggler, she attracted attention in church. She couldn't help it, she just couldn't sit still. If she wasn't swinging her legs, she'd be kicking kneelers, or fiddling with the little stack of prayer and hymn books provided.

One Sunday, Snort craned round to see who was sitting in the pew behind us, only to lock stares with the disapproving eyes of Matron.

"Helen Jarvis, sit still!" hissed Matron.

"Sorry, Matron," Snort whispered back.

Snort spun round to face the front, but it wasn't long before she forgot about Matron behind. She began making a tower with her hymn books and mine. I elbowed her in the ribs. Unfortunately, this caused the tower to collapse and fall to the stone floor. The other girls and members of the congregation turned their heads in our direction. I turned crimson with embarrassment.

Matron waited for Snort to pick up all the hymn books. Then she leaned forwards and tapped her shoulder with a sharp, gloved finger.

"I want to see you in my room when we get back," she hissed into Snort's ear.

9
A Tragic Ghost

"Now you've done it!" I scolded Snort as we walked back home after the church service.

Snort pulled a face.

"What do you think she'll make me do?"

"Lines, probably."

For once, Snort and I didn't dawdle at the Shell House, delaying the progress of the crocodile and earning ourselves a rebuke from Matron who was bringing up the rear. Usually, we couldn't resist gawking at it, it was so unusual. I didn't know the tragic story behind it then, but I do now.

The Shell House

The Shell House was unique. It was created and proudly tended by the owner, George Howard, who began building it in 1948, after his son, Michael, died at the tender age of 14 from meningitis.

Working meticulously with seashells gathered locally or collected from the time when he sailed the seven seas as a mariner, he lovingly decorated the front garden of his home. He created a statue of St George and the Dragon, a wishing well, windmill, church, birds, animals and figures, all from mosaics of seashells. Rumour had it that there were some valuable William Morris and William de Morgan art nouveau tiles pressed into the cement. Apparently, there was also coral plundered from the Red Sea, quartz from South Africa, rocks from Majorca and giant clams from the South Pacific.

The resulting work of art attracted tourists from far and wide, and the Shell House became the subject of postcards. Over the years, even after George Howard's death in 1986, the Shell House raised thousands of pounds for various charities.

Does the Shell House still stand? I'm afraid not, though I remember it as clearly as though I saw it yesterday. In 2003, it was demolished to make way for development. A very ordinary block of flats now stands on the site. However, a little British Pathé film clip still exists, made in 1965, showing the Shell House exactly as I would have seen it as a child.

This link will take you there:

http://www.britishpathe.com/video/shell-garden-beware-other-colour-pics-share-this-1

Apart from church, there was another dull Sunday chore we had to endure. It was the letter to our parents. We had to write home once a week and Matron checked and censored every letter before it was mailed. I discovered this the hard way. This was the original letter that I wrote:

> Dear M and D,
> We haven't really learnt anything at school this week. The buns are lovley but we had horrible Marmite Sqish twice this week and you know how I hate that. Snort is in BIG trouble because she made a noise in church. Matron is going to have words with her and she might be expeled. If she is I'm going on strike. Mrs Driver has a chawawa dog but it isn't a nice one it's called Brandy but Matron says it should be called Randy because it keeps jumping on everything even our satchels. I wish the food was nice here but we have tapioca which is like frogspawn and fish eyes. Soon we will go in the woods and do nelson's eye and so this may be the last letter you ever get from me because I might be dead.
> yours sincerley your middle daughter,
> Victoria

My letter was passed to Matron, who used a thick-nibbed pen loaded with black ink to cross out the parts she didn't approve of. The letter my parents received looked rather different from the one I had composed.

Dear M and D,
The buns are lovley. Snort made a noise in church. Mrs Driver has a chawawa dog called Brandy. We have tapioca. Soon we will go in the woods.
yours sincerley your middle daughter,
Victoria

We were just finishing writing our letters when Carrot came in. Carrot's real name was Julia, but we called her Carrot because her parents owned a market gardening business.

"Matron wants you and Dusty to go to her room *right away*," said Carrot, enjoying being the bearer of bad news. "She's in a real fizz. I bet it's because of the noise you were making in church."

Snort pulled a face, but I knew she was worried. So was I.

We tapped on Matron's door.

"Come in."

Snort and I shuffled in and stood side by side.

"You gels know exactly why you are here," began Matron. "We are all ambassadors of TH, and we must behave perfectly in public at all times."

"Yes, Matron."

"Your behaviour today in church was shocking. Helen, I want you write three hundred lines, *I must not make a noise in church*."

"Yes, Matron."

"And I have had a talk with Mrs Driver. We both agree that, until you both learn how to behave like polite, decent gels in church, and sit correctly, you two will sit away from the main congregation."

"Yes, Matron."

"Yes, Matron."

Back in the Common Room, we exhaled.

"Whew! Just three hundred lines! I thought I was going to be suspended."

"And we're going to be moved. Wonder where to?"

It was a couple of weeks before we found out where we would be seated for future services. It was on the far side of the church, well away from the main congregation in the middle, behind a particularly thick column. Above the dark wooden pews there was an arched, stained-glass window. When the sun shone, different coloured patches of light played on us. If Snort wriggled, nobody would really notice. It was perfect.

I wish I could say that Snort behaved from then on, but of course she didn't. Using the pin on her Shackleton house badge, she began to scrape and carve the word 'Snort' in the pew. Nobody noticed. It took her weeks and when it was finally finished, Matron called us back into her room. I was full of dread. I was positive that her graffiti had been discovered, but I was wrong.

"Well done, you two gels," said Matron. "You've been so quiet and good, Mrs Driver and I think you've earned the privilege of sitting with the others again."

We weren't pleased. No longer could I carry a novel in my pocket to read during the service, and Snort's carving days were over. I often wonder if anybody noticed her name carved into the wood, and wonder if it is still there today. And I wonder if the people who see the single word 'Snort' are baffled as to what it might mean.

Punishments usually took the form of writing lines which was boring and inconvenient, but not too ghastly. However, if a girl was *really* naughty, there were other punishments.

Sometimes we had to learn passages from Shakespeare and recite them in the prefects' room.

But perhaps the worst punishment was not being allowed home on an exeat weekend. And if anybody was caught talking after lights-out three times, she was told to strip her bed and go to the top floor, opposite Mrs Driver's suite of rooms. On the other side of the hallway was a door that led to a narrow corridor, with tiny rooms opening either side of it. These must have been servant rooms long ago, but were now occupied by prefects.

Except for one room.

Matron would unlock the door to reveal a room with nothing in it but a bed, a mattress and a pillow. The unfortunate girl would have to make up the bed and spend the night in the room. It wasn't the solitary confinement that was the problem, it was the ghost of Emily, the scullery maid.

The legend of Emily changed a little every year as it was told to the new intake of girls and embroidered upon. In my first year, when one of the older girls, Mops, told it, the story ran like this:

More than a hundred years ago, Emily was a pretty servant girl who worked in the kitchen. Emily was a hard worker, much valued by Mrs Crittle, the cook.

But Emily's mind was not completely on her work. She had noticed Thomas, the young groom who helped take care of the carriages and horses.

When Thomas knocked on the kitchen door, she made sure she was the one who answered. When Thomas ate with the servants at the kitchen table, Emily was the one who served him and smiled prettily when he thanked her.

Before long, Thomas was smitten. He couldn't stop staring at Emily. Emily felt the same and their eyes would meet across the kitchen table. When their skin touched accidentally, sparks flew.

Of course the lovers weren't allowed to spend time together, but somehow, they managed. They knew that if Mrs Crittle, or Giles, the head groom, found out, there would be enormous trouble, and they probably would lose their jobs. But the couple was careful and snatched minutes together here and there and met in secret, often at night.

Although Emily's little room was on the top floor, there was a fire escape, which she often skipped down into the arms of her lover waiting below. Together they would melt into the woods while the house slept.

All went well until one terrible night when somebody spotted the couple in the woods together. They reported the sighting to Giles, who summoned Thomas immediately.

"I'm giving you just one last chance," said Giles, wagging his finger in Thomas's face. "I order you to stop meeting the scullery maid or you will lose your job."

"But, sir! I love Emily! We want to get married!"

"It's against the rules, you know that. If Mrs Crittle finds out, Emily will lose her job, too."

"But Emily is pregnant!" Thomas blurted out, then clapped his hand over his mouth.

"What?" bellowed Giles. "Then you give me no choice, young man! Collect your things and be gone. There is no job for you here any longer."

Thomas begged and pleaded, but his entreaties fell on stony ears. His few personal possessions were thrown together and he was taken away in a carriage into the night.

By now, Mrs Crittle had heard the news and steam was coming out of her ears. Furiously, she threw open Emily's door.

"Pack your belongings, girl! I can't even bear to look at you! I thought you were grateful for your job, but you've been seeing that groom on the sly! He's gone already, and good riddance!"

"Thomas? Thomas has gone?" quavered Emily, the colour draining from her face.

"Yes, you'll never see him again."

Emily's eyes widened.

"Thomas!" she cried. "Wait for me! I'm coming!"

Before anybody could stop her, she ran barefoot past Mrs Crittle and out onto the fire escape, still wearing her long, flannel nightdress.

"Thomas! Thomas!"

Only owls answered her.

Nobody knows if Emily missed her footing on the fire escape, or whether she jumped. As she lay in a crumpled heap below, her nightdress slowly stained red. She was already dead when they reached her.

They laid Emily the scullery maid out in the room on the top floor which had been her bedroom. They placed a wooden cross in her hands, hands that were whiter than the flour in the kitchen.

But Emily never found peace. Her ghost can be seen on the upper floor of the building, or climbing down the fire escape in her long white nightgown, sobbing, looking for Thomas, the father of her unborn child.

"Did you see the ghost of Emily the scullery maid?" I asked Snort when she'd spent a night in the isolation room for being caught talking after lights-out three times.

"Nah, of course not," she said scornfully. "I went to sleep straightaway, but I did dream about Nelson's Eye. I wish they'd hurry up and get it over with."

Saturday mornings were taken up with compulsory sport plus another Prep session, although the afternoon was largely free. This was the day Snort and I disappeared into the woods that comprised TH's grounds. The woodland was well-established and sturdy metal railings marked the boundary. However, we were never permitted to walk right up to the boundary.

"When you gels go into the woods, you are not allowed past the trees that have a white ring painted on them," Matron told us on our first day.

"Why not?" asked Snort.

"Never you mind," said Matron. "That's the rule, beyond the white-ringed trees is out of bounds. And if I catch any gels breaking that rule, they will be severely punished."

It didn't take long for us to find out why we weren't allowed past the white rings. Snort asked one of the older girls.

"Flashers," she replied without hesitation.

"Oh, I see," said Snort, although she didn't.

So I asked my older sister, who knew exactly what they were.

"Flashers? You know, bad men who get their thingies out and wave them about."

"Oh!"

Snort and I looked at each other and dissolved into giggles.

Unfortunately, it was true. As TH was a girls' school, it was a mecca for flashers. Many were reported, but by the time the police arrived, they had vanished.

One Saturday afternoon, Snort and I had changed into our shorts and were carrying a blanket and a box of comics, heading for the woods. It was a warm day and we didn't feel like joining in with the game of Tin Can Bosh that others in our dorm had been planning around the area in the woods we called Pug's Hole. Instead, we headed in the opposite direction. Suddenly, a group of older girls jumped out at us from behind some rhododendron bushes.

"It's time!" they said, grabbing our arms.

"Stop it! Let go!" we squeaked. "Time for what?"

But Snort and I both knew and our hearts were filled with dread. It was time for Nelson's Eye.

Cauliflower Cheese

Serves 4

Medium head of cauliflower, broken into large florets
40g (1½ oz) butter
40g (1½ oz) plain flour
400ml (14 fl oz) milk
1 tsp English mustard
100g (3½ oz) mature cheddar cheese, grated
Salt and freshly ground black pepper

Method
- Preheat the oven to 190C/375F/Gas Mark 5.
- Thoroughly wash the cauliflower and place in a large saucepan of salted water.
- Bring to the boil and cook for 5 minutes ensuring that the cauliflower is still fairly firm.
- Tip into a colander and leave to drain.
- Melt the butter in a saucepan and stir in the flour.
- Cook over a gentle heat for one minute.
- Remove the pan from the heat and gradually add the milk, a little at a time, stirring well.
- Return the pan to a medium heat and bring the mixture to the boil, stirring constantly. Simmer for two minutes, then remove from the heat.
- Stir in the mustard and two thirds of the cheese, and set aside. Arrange the cauliflower in an ovenproof baking dish. Carefully pour over the sauce, ensuring the cauliflower is completely covered.
- Scatter the remaining cheese over and bake for 25-30 minutes, until the top is golden-brown and bubbling.

10
Nelson's Eye

The rug and box we were carrying dropped to the ground and the comics spilled out.

"Nelson's Eye! Nelson's Eye!" chanted the older girls as they blindfolded us with woollen TH scarves wound around our heads.

I lost track of where Snort was when my shoulders were held, and I was spun round and round. Then I was half-pushed, half-led, deeper into the woods. I deduced that from the fact that the leaf litter seemed thicker underfoot, and low branches scraped me.

"Where are you taking us?" I asked, stumbling.

"Silence! You are not allowed to talk during Nelson's Eye!"

From the whispers, I guessed there were about three girls steering me. It seemed like a long walk. The woods were not flat; there were huge dips and sudden drops, like Pug's Hole, a favourite place for us girls to play. Underground air-raid shelters had been built during World War II but these were now overgrown, leaving humps in the ground that we either climbed over or navigated round. The journey seemed to take forever. Twigs snapped underfoot and startled birds squawked and flapped away. Brambles scratched my bare legs. At last we stopped and I wondered whether Snort was nearby.

"Who are you?" shouted a girl.

I stood still. Was she talking to me?

"Who are you?" shouted the girl again. "Answer me!"

"Answer her!" somebody hissed in my ear.

"I'm Dusty, well, my real name's Vic..." I started, but was cut short.

"No, you're not! You are the lowest cabin girl on the ship! You are lower than the ship's cat! Even lower than a rat! Until you pass the initiation ceremony, you will have no name!"

I stood still, listening.

"Are you ready, Nameless?"

"Er, yes."

"Do you agree to take the test, Nameless?"

"Yes." *What choice did I have?*

"Do you promise never to talk of the ceremony of Nelson's Eye to anyone, ever?"

"I promise."

"If you do, you will be cursed, and the ghost of Emily the scullery maid will haunt you until the day you leave the school. Say you promise."

"I promise."

"And who are you?" shouted the girl in another direction.

"I'm nameless too," said Snort's voice from some distance away.

She had clearly heard my interchange, and she was a quick learner.

"Correct! You are nameless and you are the lowest cabin girl on the ship! You are lower than the ship's cat! Even lower than a rat! Do you promise *never* to speak of Nelson's Eye to anyone, ever? And do you understand that if you do, you will be cursed, and the ghost of Emily the scullery maid will haunt you until the day you leave TH?"

I held my breath. Snort was not one to be bossed around, and I knew she didn't believe in the ghost of Emily the scullery maid. A slight pause.

"Yes. I promise."

Whew! Well done, Snort. Best to play along.

"Then let the ceremony commence!"

"Nelson's Eye! Nelson's Eye! Nelson's Eye! Nelson's Eye!"

From all around me, I could hear the chanting, so I guessed we were in a clearing filled with older girls.

"Shake hands with the skeleton of Nelson!"

I stood still, not understanding.

"Go on then, shake hands!" someone urged.

I stuck my right hand out, grasped the skeletal hand, and shook it. It was so obviously a tree branch I almost laughed. I hoped Snort would behave.

"Now shake the hand of a corpse that has been floating in the ocean."

Obediently, I shook hands with what felt like a rubber glove filled with water. Easy.

"These are Nelson's kidneys, squeeze them in your hands."

Bleugh! Now that didn't sound very nice. Gingerly, I held out my hands, palms up. Two peeled boiled eggs were plopped into them. I knew exactly what they were as soon as I felt them and squeezed them with no trouble at all.

"Now it's time to walk the plank! When you get to the end, you must jump. Be careful, it's a long way down."

Now I really *was* scared. Where were we? Were we near Pug's Hole? If so, that was a really steep drop in the woods. I knew there was no water as I didn't think we were anywhere near the Bug Pond, but how far would I have to jump?

"Walk, Nameless!"

What if I broke a leg and had to stay in the Sanatorium, like Broomhead in Upper Four, who broke her leg in gym and couldn't climb the stairs to her dorm?

"Walk-the-plank, walk-the-plank, walk-the-plank," chanted the spectators.

I felt for the beginning of the plank with the toe of my sandal. Thankfully, the plank was wide. I shuffled slowly along it, arms outstretched to keep balance, desperately wishing I could rip the blindfold away from my eyes and see where I was going.

"Walk! Walk! Walk!" chanted the spectators, more excited now.

I shuffled further.

"You are at the end now, stop!"

I stopped.

"Now jump!"

I knew I had to, but I really didn't want to jump. My legs were trembling.

"Jump! Jump! Jump!" shouted the spectators.

I took a deep breath, bent my knees and sprang high into the air off the end of the board.

There was no drop at all. The plank was flat on the ground, not suspended above any drop. Apart from the shock, and stumbling a little as I landed, I was totally unhurt and would not need carting off to the Sanatorium. The relief was immeasurable.

I must have looked very silly, and I could hear laughter, quickly muffled because they were about to play the same trick on Snort.

"And finally, you must plunge your finger into Nelson's eye!"

After walking the plank, this shouldn't be a problem. Easy-peasy, lemon squeezy.

My hand was grasped, and my extended forefinger was pushed into something wet and squelchy. It was extremely unpleasant, but not painful.

Then the scarf over my eyes was pulled off. It was over!

As I blinked in the sudden light, I discovered what I had pushed my finger into: a mouldy orange. I wiped off the mess on my finger on the back of my shorts. There were plenty of girls in the clearing, including some girls from my dorm. I opened my mouth to speak, but they all put their fingers to their lips, and pointed. It was Snort's turn to walk the plank.

Poor Snort. I knew how she was feeling, but she was braver than me and didn't hesitate. She jumped off the end of the plank as soon as she was told and was just as surprised as me to discover that the ground was level. Nelson's mouldy eye gave her no trouble either.

"You have both passed the ceremony," said the girl whose voice was by now familiar to us. "I hereby name you Dusty and Snort!"

The spectators applauded. The relief was enormous. Nelson's Eye was no longer a black cloud that hung over us. We had done it, passed it, and survived.

"I'm so glad that's over," I said to Snort when we were alone again.

"Me too! Most of it was just silly, but I hated walking the plank."

I nodded, recalling my fear.

I suppose we were lucky really. Initiation ceremonies are common in English public schools, particularly boys' schools, and Nelson's Eye was very mild compared with some.

My brother told me that every new boy in some schools had to crawl under all the beds in the dorm, getting thwacked with slippers as they emerged from under each bed. Some schools pushed new boys in laundry baskets down flights of steps. Ritual cold baths were administered at others, or 'crucifixions' where a broom pole was pushed through the sleeves of a blazer like a scarecrow, while the unlucky new boy was wearing it.

"I thought we might end up in the San with broken legs," I said.

The Sanatorium (or San) was housed in a separate building and was Sister MacDonald's empire. It looked rather like a dorm, except it was sterile and devoid of any personality, much like any hospital ward.

Sister MacDonald was a large, fierce lady who rustled as she moved. Her white uniform was starched so stiffly that it surprised me that it allowed her to walk at all, and I was sure she couldn't sit down.

Sister MacDonald's main purpose in life seemed to be to track down malingerers and send them back to school immediately. Unless a girl had a broken limb, or a ridiculously high temperature, or was covered in spots that the doctor pronounced contagious, she was perfectly fit to go back to school, in Sister MacDonald's opinion.

Sister MacDonald had a fool-proof test she would apply to all suspected malingerers. It went like this:

Sister MacDonald: Would you like a nice bowl of ice cream?
Patient: No, thank you.
Sister MacDonald: Poor dear, lie down and get some rest.

or

Sister MacDonald: Would you like a nice bowl of ice cream?
Patient: Yes, please!
Sister MacDonald: Right, up you get and get dressed. I'm discharging you now. If you hurry, you'll catch afternoon lessons.

❀ ❀ ❀

School Report

English: Victoria is keen but her work is spoilt by carelessness.

Mathematics: If Victoria made more effort to concentrate instead of staring out of the window, we would all see better results.

Victoria has made a disappointing start. She must learn to set a good example, always behave in public and not be a leader in rule breaking. Her untidiness is proverbial.

Mrs Driver (Housemistress)

❋ ❋ ❋

Boarding school wasn't a bit like Enid Blyton had described it, but I still quite enjoyed it. We didn't have many midnight feasts as the threat, if caught, of sleeping in the isolation room with Emily the scullery maid, was not attractive.

There was also another strange tradition that was never mentioned in Enid Blyton's books: namely, GOs. The abbreviation GO stood for Gone On, and each new junior was supposed to choose a senior girl to be 'gone on'. That meant you had a crush on her and you were supposed to write her little notes and swoon every time you saw her.

I chose Shirley, a friend of my sister's. I don't remember who Snort chose, but you were only allowed to choose somebody that nobody else had already chosen. It was a strange, rather pointless tradition, perhaps a little akin to 'fagging' without the harshness. Fagging, in many boarding schools, meant younger pupils were required to act as personal servants to senior pupils and were often disciplined severely. Thankfully, as far as I knew, nothing like that happened at TH.

Some girls in my dorm suffered terribly from homesickness, but I wasn't one of those. Of course, I couldn't have Prince Snowy Twinkletoes with me, which was sad. I wished our school was like some others that allowed pets. But I did have Snort as a friend, and my older sister, should I ever need her.

We looked forward to exeats, when we could go home for the day, but these were over so fast there was barely time to do anything. During these visits, I remember how small my house and bedroom seemed as I'd grown accustomed to the long corridors of St Mary's and our large dorm. I was so used to sharing a dorm that, in the holidays, it felt strange to be the only person sleeping in a room.

But Enid Blyton described the camaraderie well. We girls grew very close and Snort and I were inseparable. Our days were crammed full and we were never bored. Almost every minute was accounted for in some way, right down to Thursday evenings when we were allowed to watch part of Top of the Pops in the portacabin, the only room with a TV, apart from Matron's and Mrs Driver's rooms. We could only watch part of the show as it coincided with bedtime, which was set in stone.

I've always been a good sleeper and in those days, I was usually asleep as soon as my head hit the pillow. The ghost of Emily the scullery maid could have danced a highland fling on the end of my bed and I probably wouldn't have woken up. One time, Snort had a bad cold and began to snore, but I wasn't the one who threw slippers at her because I slept right through it.

One week, Matron rather pointedly pinned up a plan on the door of the dorm. It was a map of St Mary's showing the nearest fire exits.

"Well, that's easy," said Snort. "If there's a fire, we just dash down the stairs, through the locker room and out of the back door."

"Correct," said Matron, then added darkly, "but what if that route was blocked?"

We had a think about that.

"And mind you gels read the rules at the bottom of the sheet."

Matron left, and Snort read the rules aloud. We listened carefully.

Do not take any possessions with you, even items of value or teddies.
Put on slippers or shoes and a pair of linings.
Vacate the dorm in a single orderly line.
The Dorm Captain should be the last to leave, having made sure everyone is out.

Unsurprisingly, that very night, a fire drill took place.

Rrrrrrrrrrrrrinnnngggg...

"Dusty! Wake up! It's a fire drill!"

"Wh…"

Snort had been voted Dorm Captain, probably much to Matron and Mrs Driver's dismay, as she was the most unruly girl in the dorm.

"Quick," shouted Snort. "Put your knickers on! And your slippers! Hurry up! Everybody out!"

I was heading the line, but to my surprise, the flight of stairs leading down to our nearest exit was blocked. Shirley, my GO, was standing there holding up a large piece of paper saying FLAMES.

"Oh, Shirley!" I said, pretending to swoon, the behaviour expected when one met one's GO.

"Not now!" she hissed. "Quick, you'll have to go up the next flight of stairs, along the corridor past Mrs Driver's room and down the stairs on the far side."

I turned and led the line up the stairs. However, outside Mrs Driver's room was another prefect holding up a sign saying FLAMES. I had no choice but to turn right and led the line into the back corridor that housed the isolation room and was haunted by Emily the scullery maid. Our slippers clumped along the bare floorboards until we reached the big window that opened onto the fire escape. Out we climbed, one by one, and clattered down the very fire escape where Emily was said to have met her tragic death.

"Well done, gels," said Matron when we reached the bottom. "And I'm very pleased to see you all remembered to put on your linings."

Now I understood why we had to put on our underwear. If it had been a real fire, the firemen would have gained more than an eyeful as we girls descended that fire escape.

Within ten minutes, we were back in the dorm, in bed and dozing off to sleep again.

However, there was one particular night when every girl and member of staff was wide awake in the middle of the night, and it had nothing at all to do with fire drills.

11
Bad Boys

As we climbed into our beds one moonlit night, we had no idea of the spectacle we were about to witness.

"Goodnight, gels," said Matron at the doorway of the dorm as she switched off the light as usual. "No more talking now."

"Goodnight, Matron," we chorused.

We drifted off to sleep as owls screeched to each other in the woods. By midnight, all the girls and staff would have been asleep. It was a warm, still, summer night, with just the occasional cloud sliding across the moon, throwing the world into momentary darkness. As the hand of the clock clicked round into the small hours, St Mary's lay silent and peaceful. Until...

Vroooooom! Vroooooom!

Night sounds always seem louder, but this noise was deafening, and growing louder by the second. Even we young girls couldn't sleep through that. We sat up, wide awake.

"What on earth?"

Vroooooom! Vroooooom!

Snort sprang out of bed and ran to the window, tugging the curtain aside.

Vroooooom! Vroooooom!

"Oh golly! Quick, come and SEE!"

We leapt out of bed and pressed our faces against the glass, then gaped. Outside, on the drive, six or seven motorbikes were idling, ridden by *boys!*

Suddenly, the dorm door was thrown open, framing Matron. I didn't know whether to stare at her in her pink quilted dressing gown, with rows of curlers in her hair, or at the scene outside.

"Gels! Stay in the dorm, we are dealing with the situation. And come away from the windows."

With that, she turned on her fluffy high-heeled slippers and clacked off down the stairs.

Come away from the windows? She may as well have asked us to recite the alphabet in Icelandic whilst standing on our heads. No way could we tear ourselves away from watching the events outside with the *boys!*

The motorcyclists had paused in a line, their engines still rumbling. They sat astride their machines, one foot on the ground, looking up at our building. I followed their gaze. Every dorm was awake, every curtain drawn open, every window had faces staring out, even the prefects' windows. The motorcyclists waved cheekily, revved their engines and roared out of sight round the building.

"They're leaving," said Corky, disappointment in her voice, as the noise of the engines grew fainter.

But she was mistaken. The boys merely circled the building, and in seconds they were back below us, slowing to wave to their adoring audience of girls, standing at the windows above. Round and round they roared, until suddenly, just as they reached the steps up to our entrance door again and slowed to wave, the front door was wrenched open. We gasped.

There stood Mrs Driver dressed in a pair of green tartan pyjamas and waving a furled umbrella.

"Go away, you're trespassing!" she shouted, shaking her fist.

The youths probably couldn't hear what she was saying over the engine noise, but her wrath was clear. However, it had no effect on them whatsoever. They merely grinned and set off on another circuit.

"Hurrah!" we cheered, loving the excitement.

Matron appeared behind Mrs Driver, just as the motorcycles completed another lap and skidded to a halt.

"I have called the police!" shouted Matron, her hands cupped like a megaphone.

The boys laughed, and waved at the girls in the windows, who waved back. Then they revved up and shot off on yet another circuit.

Mrs Driver and Matron were livid. Together they marched out into the middle of the drive and stretched out their arms, as if to bar the way. Round swept the motorbikes. But they didn't hesitate; they appeared to be heading straight for the crazy-looking woman in green tartan pyjamas and the other in the pink dressing gown and slippers, with rows of curlers in her hair.

"Gosh, they're brave!" said Snort, as we watched the confrontation.

The bikers hardly checked their speed. They headed straight for the two women, but at the last second, peeled off sideways, swerving onto the grassed area, thus avoiding any collision.

Dozens of girls at the windows exhaled. This was better than any movie, even the latest ones like *Coolhand Luke* or *Bonnie and Clyde*.

Mrs Driver and Matron were a formidable duo. As the motorbikes swept round again, the ladies tried again to become human barricades, doing their best to obstruct the approaching machines. The boys narrowly missed them and began another lap.

In our dorm, nobody had said a word for ages; we were too engrossed in the scene below. Many of us had our hands clapped over our mouths in disbelief.

I don't know who or what lent Mrs Driver such courage that night, although I could hazard a guess judging from the slight sway in her walk. Whatever, when the motorbikes circled for a third time, she was purple with rage. As they neared her, she leaped out in an attempt to physically seize one of the trespassers. He swerved and successfully avoided Mrs Driver and her umbrella. At the same time, we suddenly heard distant police sirens.

The boys decided that the game was over for the night. They really didn't want to face the crazy suicidal, tartan pyjama clad harridan again, neither did they want to spend a night in a police cell. With a last wave to their adoring fans at the windows, they turned and headed their bikes down the drive towards the campus entrance gates.

But Lady Luck wasn't smiling on one of the bikers. He was so intent on waving to his female audience, he didn't realise how close Mrs Driver was to her quarry. Her eyes narrowed, and she launched herself at him.

All the girls in our dorm, and probably all the girls in the other dorms and prefects' rooms, gasped. The other motorbikes had already accelerated out of the grounds and vanished. The police sirens were markedly closer.

Mrs Driver's rugby tackle didn't quite connect, but it was enough to unnerve the young man, who lost control of the bike, sending it into an uncontrollable wobble. The bike wasn't travelling fast, but Mrs Driver was.

"I've got you, boy!" she yelled, lunging at him and grabbing at his jacket.

In horror, the youth dropped his motorbike on the ground and fled towards the woods, with Mrs Driver in hot pursuit.

"Come back here, boy!" she shouted.

But the lad had no intentions of doing anything of the sort. He disappeared into the woods, his black leather-clad figure instantly melting into the shadows. Mrs Driver was quite a big woman, and although out of breath, she didn't give up. Seconds later, she, too, was swallowed up by the woods as a convoy of police cars with screaming sirens and blue flashing lights screeched to a halt outside St Mary's. The abandoned motorbike on the grass had stalled, but one wheel was still spinning.

Policemen leaped out of the cars leaving the doors hanging open. Matron, holding her dressing gown together at the throat with one hand, used the other to point a long finger at the woods. The policemen turned and ran into the trees.

"This is better than Tom and Jerry," said Snort. "I hope he gets away."

Nothing happened for a long time. Gradually faces disappeared from the windows as there was nothing to see except the blue lights flashing on the roofs of the police cars. Matron went inside and did a round of the dorms, ordering us all back to bed.

"Settle down now, gels," she said, drawing the curtains firmly. "It's all over."

Snort and I waited until her slippers had clacked away up the corridor, then we slipped out of bed again and peeped through the gap in the curtain.

We had to wait quite a long time. We heard owls, and saw bats flitting round the lamp that lit the steps to the entrance, but there was no sign of the man-hunt. We were just about to give up, when a procession emerged from the woods. It was headed by two policemen, one handcuffed to the sorry youth, who was black with dirt. Next came a line of more policemen, looking satisfied with themselves, pleased that their quarry had been apprehended. And finally, the familiar figure of Mrs Driver, in her tartan pyjamas, and picking the odd pine needle out of her hair, brought up the rear.

The youth was put into the back of a police car, the policemen climbed into their cars, and the whole convoy pulled away. Mrs Driver came back into St Mary's and I heard her climb the steps to her floor, muttering darkly to herself. The young man's motorbike was left lying on the ground, but somebody collected it the next day.

"Matron, how did they catch the boy in the woods?" asked Snort the next day.

"Never you gels mind. The important thing is that they caught him."

However, we *did* learn how the youth had been caught, but not from Matron or Mrs Driver. It so happened that one of the Day Bugs had an uncle in the police force, and he'd been called out to the incident. According to him, this is what happened.

The young man fled into the woods, with Mrs Driver close behind. The boy zig-zagged through the trees but the incensed Mrs Driver somehow kept up. In spite of the moon, it was dark, and the boy was not familiar with the layout of the woods. He made a bad mistake. As he looked over his shoulder to sense how close Mrs Driver was, he didn't see Pug's Hole opening out in front of him. He fell down the steep incline. Mrs Driver couldn't stop in time, lost her footing and also toppled down the slope.

At the bottom, the two looked at each other for a brief second.

"I've got you now!" crowed Mrs Driver, grabbing his arm.

"Oh no, you haven't," he said, wriggling out of her grasp and jumping back onto his feet.

The chase continued. Mrs Driver was more than twice the lad's age, and was soon out of breath and wheezing. The boy was probably tired of being hunted down, and frightened by the police sirens. He changed tactics. As Mrs Driver stopped to catch her breath, he caught sight of an air raid shelter and decided to hide from her and the Law. When a cloud obscured the moon briefly, the lad tugged up the manhole cover, which opened surprisingly easily considering its age and the soil and vegetation that had collected on it. He quickly climbed in and down the ladder, quietly closing the manhole cover behind him.

Unfortunately for the trespasser, Mrs Driver had seen where he went.

It can't have been very nice inside the ancient air raid shelter, pitch black, crawling with spiders and who knows what else. And matters didn't improve when Mrs Driver stood on the cover.

"Haha, I've caught you now!" she cried, dancing a crazy little jig on the lid.

I imagine the movement showered loose soil and filth onto the poor lad below.

The police arrived with flashlights to see Mrs Driver still dancing on the manhole cover.

"We'll take over from here," said a policeman. "I can see you've caught the suspect."

Reluctantly, Mrs Driver stepped aside.

The policeman bent down and raised the cover. He shone his torch down into the darkness.

"Hello, we have you surrounded," he called down. "Are you ready to come up with your hands in the air?"

"Yes!" echoed the youth's voice from below. "As long as you protect me from that madwoman in tartan pyjamas!"

As meek as a woodland mouse, the boy scrambled back up the ladder. A couple of officers stood close to Mrs Driver to make sure she didn't try to take the law into her own hands. As soon as the youth climbed out, the policeman clapped handcuffs on him, and that was that.

I don't believe the boy or his accomplices were ever charged. I hope not, because their offence wasn't serious, and it provided huge entertainment for us girls. Shortly after, I believe the gates into the campus were locked nightly, so nothing like that ever happened again while I was there.

I was very happy at TH. When her time came, my sister elected to leave, attend college and live at home. I didn't think it would affect me, but I was in for a big surprise. When my parents arrived to take us home for the holidays, along with the trunks for packing, they brought shocking news.

12
Summer Break

Packing our trunks for the holidays was so much easier than packing for the start of a new term. All we had to do was throw stuff in, with no need to check the inventory carefully. However, there always seemed to be more to take home than we had initially brought.

"I can't get it to shut," I said. "Snort, come and sit on this side."

Snort obliged and the trunk snapped shut.

"Well, that's it," I said. "I'm not opening it again. If I've forgotten anything, I'll just have to collect it next term."

"*Ach*, well, that's the thing," said my mother. "We've decided that as your sister is no longer here, it would be better for us all if you went to day school closer to home."

My jaw dropped and I sat heavily on the trunk beside Snort.

"Dusty's leaving?" asked Snort.

"Yes, Helen, she is. But of course you two must see each other during the holidays, lots of times…"

I was heartbroken, and so was Snort, but the decision had been made. Looking back on it now, I imagine it was probably more of a financial decision as my father had just retired from the army.

I never saw Snort again. Her parents lived in Singapore, so we couldn't meet in the holidays. We wrote letters for a while, but as our lives progressed, the letters faded and finally died away.

I tried to put the thought of starting at a new school behind me and concentrated on enjoying my summer break. The first week was always tricky as my parents opened our end of term reports. As usual, my sister's positively glowed, while mine was a little worse than mediocre.

❀ ❀ ❀

School Report

English: Victoria may have ability but this is not evident as she is disorganised, untidy and rarely produces homework.

Mathematics: Victoria's defeatist attitude and daydreaming do not assist her progress in this subject.

It would seem that Victoria has made very little progress this term. Unless her overall attitude improves, it is unlikely that Victoria will succeed in her new school. However, we wish her well.

❀ ❀ ❀

It was fortunate for me that my younger brother's school report was even worse than mine. The comments from his teachers were so appalling that my parents decided to send him to a 'crammer' the next term. A crammer is a school that prepares pupils for examinations. I felt sorry for him, but pleased that my report was marginally better than his.

It wasn't my happiest time. I felt settled at boarding school and I missed Snort already. I was thirteen and I couldn't even imagine going to a new school and having to start all over again. At one point, I even considered running away, although I'm not sure how I thought that would help the situation. What I actually did was *pretend* to run away, just to see if anybody cared. I shut myself in the outside toilet, a place nobody used as it was a home for spiders.

"*Ach,* where has Victoria gone?" I heard my mother say on her way down the garden to visit her beloved compost heap.

"Probably gone round to see Annabel," said my brother.

I held my breath, waiting. Were they worried? Would they go round to Auntie Jean's and check? Nobody did, and I got very bored waiting in the toilet. Eventually, I shuffled out. Nobody commented because nobody had realised I'd gone missing. It was a huge non-event.

Of course my pride was dented, but I soon forgot about it as I helped make Crispy Crunchy Crackly Crack with Auntie Jean and Annabel in their kitchen. Oh, the pleasure of that first bite and taste with a glass of milk! It was enough to make anybody forget all about running away.

Auntie Jean was a wonderful cook, unlike my mother. I think my mother could have been, but her plants interested her far more.

Crispy Crunchy Crackly Crack

Ingredients
50g (2 oz) butter
1 tablespoon cocoa powder
1 tablespoon golden syrup
Raisins (optional)
50g (2 oz) crushed digestive biscuits
Cooking chocolate (optional)

Method
Prep: 20min
Extra time: 4hr chilling
- Melt the butter in a non-stick pan.
- Add in the cocoa powder, golden syrup and raisins (optional).
- When the ingredients blend to make a brown, sticky liquid, remove from the heat.
- Add in the crushed digestive biscuits.
- Mix and put in a 18cm (7in) square baking tin and leave in fridge until it becomes hard, probably about 4 hours.
- Pour melted chocolate over the chocolate biscuit cake.
- Cut into small squares.

However, sometimes a glut in the garden would spur her into making slightly crazy dishes, her Eastern European heritage making a rare appearance.

"*Ach*, the plums are nearly ripe. Next week we will make *Zwetschgenknödel*."

"Hooray!"

Zwetschgenknödel (plum dumplings)

For 16 dumplings

4 tablespoons butter
1 cup dry bread crumbs
4 large russet potatoes, peeled
2 cups plain, all-purpose flour
1 egg
1 pinch salt
16 ripe plums, pitted or left whole (damson plums or Italian prune plums are best, but any plum will work)
16 teaspoons white sugar, one tsp for each dumpling. Or 16 sugar cubes.

Method

- Melt 3 tablespoons of butter in a skillet over medium-low heat. Throw in the bread crumbs. Cook and stir until golden brown and fragrant, about 2 minutes. Set the crumbs aside.
- Place potatoes in a pot of water over medium heat, and boil until tender, 20 to 30 minutes. Drain the potatoes, and allow to cool for several minutes to dry out; then squeeze the potatoes through a fine sieve or potato ricer into a bowl.
- Place 1 tablespoon of butter into the potatoes, and allow to melt, then mix in the flour until thoroughly combined. Mix in egg and salt. Turn the mixture out onto a generously floured work surface, and knead until the dough is soft and no longer sticky, about 10 minutes.
- Divide the dough into quarters, and subdivide each quarter into fourths to make 16 portions. Roll each portion into a ball, and roll the ball out on a floured work surface until it forms a circle about 9cm (3½ inches) in diameter. Place a pitted plum into the center of the dough circle, and spoon a teaspoon of sugar into the plum. Alternatively, pit the plum and insert a sugar cube into each plum. Roll and pinch the dough around the plum to seal. Repeat with the remaining dough to make 16 dumplings.
- Bring a pot of lightly salted water to a boil over medium heat, and drop the dumplings into the boiling water. Stir gently to loosen any dumplings that stick to the bottom. Allow the dumplings to rise to the top, then boil for 5 more minutes.
- Gently remove dumplings with a slotted spoon, and roll in the toasted bread crumbs to serve.
- Any remaining dough can be rolled into plain dumplings, boiled, and rolled in crumbs.

The damson plums ripened, and the day was set aside for *Zwetschgenknödel*, or plum dumplings.

On these days, we all lent a hand. My brother and I rushed out into the garden and picked the plums from the tree, dodging the wasps that were just as keen to get to the fruit as we were. Then we washed the plums, but, unlike most recipes, left the stones in. My sister was on dough duty, and my mother supervised and dropped the dumplings into boiling water. The result was a mountain of fragrant dumplings. On *Zwetschgenknödel* days, there was nothing else on the menu; we just guzzled *Zwetschgenknödel*, eating them with our hands, juice running down our faces. We ate until we could eat no more.

My mother's gardening skills ensured we had fresh vegetables and fruit nearly all year round. The only thing she failed dismally at was corn on the cob. The cobs never reached their full size, and never ripened to that glorious yellow. This was a big disappointment, particularly as my parents had named the house *Kukuruz*, meaning corn on the cob. I really don't know why it was named that. When the subject came up, my parents would steal secret glances at each other and my mother would blush.

Along with gardening, history was another of my mother's passions.

"Come along!" she would shout up the stairs. "Today we are visiting Sherborne Castle. It was built by Sir Walter Raleigh, you know, and it has 40 acres of grounds."

We climbed into Ivy, and she ground the gears and bucked all the way to Sherborne, some 40 miles away.

My mother adored visiting castles and country estates, all steeped in history, then touring the grounds, always on the lookout for gardening ideas. Dorset has numerous stately homes, and we probably visited most of them. I don't remember many individually; they blur together in a haze of suits of armour, portraits, mazes and kitchen gardens.

I remember visiting Athelhampton House, a fine example of a 15th century manor house surrounded by one of the great architectural gardens of England. Of course, my mother almost drooled as she spotted rare plants, and her sleight of hand, as she stole cuttings and stashed them in her enormous handbag, was legendary.

I also recall Kingston Lacy, an elegant Italian-inspired country residence in Wimborne Minster. I don't remember it because of its lavish interior, or because of its splendid gardens. I remember it because of the rather incongruous Egyptian obelisk, sculpted from pink granite, which stands in the gardens.

In 1820, adventurer William John Bankes found the toppled 2nd century BC obelisk on the Nile island of Philae. Being a collector, he arranged to have the granite artefact transported to his family home in Dorset. The inscriptions on this obelisk, along with the famous Rosetta Stone, helped crack open the mystery of the ancient Egyptian symbols.

And the story didn't finish there. Very recently, in 2014 to be precise, the inscriptions were inspected again. Modern imaging techniques allowed for areas to be deciphered that had gradually been rubbed away by centuries of Egyptian sun and 200 years of English weather. The result has revealed startling new insights into ancient Egyptian history. Fifty years later, Joe and I visited the island of Philae on the Nile, the birthplace of the Kingston Lacy obelisk I had stared at as a child.

Back home, my mother nurtured and nursed the cuttings and seeds she had stolen. It was common to overhear this typical conversation as she walked visitors round our garden.

"*Ach,* this rather unusual azalea comes from Athelhampton House, and this shrub here is a very fine hebe I found in the grounds of Lulworth Castle."

Another of my mother's ideas of a good time was visiting old churches, of which there were hundreds within easy reach of Ivy. Old churches abound in Dorset, and we visited many. Some were within walking distance of our house, like the Saxon St Martin's Church, which is one thousand years old and holds a priceless effigy of Lawrence of Arabia.

Why Wareham for such a valuable effigy? Because it was sculpted for St Paul's Cathedral but was refused because of the controversy surrounding T.E. Lawrence's death. Neither would Westminster Abbey or Salisbury Cathedral take it. So it ended up in the tiny Wareham church which, at a stretch, seats just 40. The effigy didn't interest me much, but I stared with horrified fascination at the crude red stars daubed on one wall, each star representing yet another death in the parish due to the Great Plague.

I confess, as a child, I didn't always enjoy these trips. The churches were dark and cold inside, and smelled musty. Even the sun shining through the stained-glass windows didn't brighten things up much. I did quite enjoy exploring the graveyards, reading the headstones with ghoulish interest, but even that palled after a while.

So my mother came up with an idea she thought might keep us amused. She bought thick wax crayons and rolls of shelf-lining paper, and showed us how to lay the paper on a headstone or brass plaque. When we rubbed the wax crayon over the surface of the paper, the inscriptions magically appeared on the paper. Brass-rubbing, as this was called, is no longer permitted as it is very damaging, but it was common in those days.

My mother's latest money-making venture, painting little salt boxes my father made with *edelweiss* flowers, (I will sell hundreds! I can't understand why nobody has thought of it before!) hadn't taken off, so she was trying something completely different. She became a market researcher, working for a big company. Now she knocked on doors asking to interview people from specific age groups, or lurked on street corners ready to pounce on unsuspecting members of the public. More and more of her time was taken up by her new job.

"*Ach*, you should take the children away somewhere," she suggested to my father, "then I can catch up with my paperwork."

Discussion followed, and a decision was made. My father would take us camping in the New Forest that weekend.

"Can Annabel come, too?"

"Not this time, we haven't got room in the tent. Now go and get your stuff together."

The tent was new, we hadn't taken it on its maiden voyage yet. Ivy was packed up with great excitement. The drive, with my father at the helm, was surprisingly smooth, with no kangaroo jumps.

The New Forest was decreed a royal forest by King William I in about 1079. Used for the royal hunt, it consisted mainly of deer, and is mentioned in the Domesday Book. Wild ponies are plentiful having been allowed to roam free and breed for centuries. In fact, as Wikipedia states:

Grazing of commoners' ponies and cattle is an essential part of the management of the Forest, helping to maintain the internationally important heathland, bog, grassland and wood-pasture habitats and their associated wildlife.

"First person to see a pony wins!" shouted my sister.

That didn't take long as the wild ponies, although unbroken, are very accustomed to humans. Not only did we see ponies, but also foals born that spring. I hugged myself in anticipation. That night, I so hoped to see deer, maybe badgers, and foxes, too. I also knew that there were still some red squirrels in the New Forest. These did finally vanish in the 1970s, chased out by their grey cousins, and only survived in cut off, managed areas like Brownsea Island.

We put the tent up eventually, although it wasn't easy. It was the type that had a separate inner bedroom. My sister and I were going to sleep in there, while my father and brother slept in the outer part. We pumped up our inflatable mattresses and laid out our sleeping bags; it all looked very cosy and inviting. The New Forest ponies watched our activities and swished their tails.

"Let's explore," I said, my notebook in hand. "I want to see some wildlife!"

13
Robberies

The campsite seemed very nice, but on my first trip to the washrooms, I made three discoveries.

- New Forest ponies watch everything you do.
- Campsite washrooms are a breeding ground for spiders. Big hairy ones.
- Campsites don't necessarily provide hot water.

Never mind. We were only there for one night and breakfast.

I'd been reading up all about the New Forest, and I knew that we should be able to spot quite a lot of wildlife. I didn't think spiders really counted.

"We'd better lock tonight's supper away in the tent," said my father. "I'm looking forward to hotdogs."

We zipped up the tent carefully and made our way down the track, equine eyes following us.

I'd love to be able to report that we saw badgers, several species of deer, stoats, red squirrels, grey squirrels, polecats and dozens of species of birds. But we didn't. Plenty of ponies, of course, but nothing else. At the end of the walk, all I could write down in my notebook was:

Spiders - in washroom
Ants - on ground, climbing trees
Beetles - on ground, climbing trees
Ponies - everywhere

A naturalist never gives up, I told myself and the watching ponies. Perhaps I'd see some wildlife during the night.

"Time to cook our supper," said my father, and we headed back to our campsite as the sun sank behind the trees.

Ponies stopped cropping the grass and lifted their heads as we passed. An annoying zing floated past my ear and I added another sighting to my list.

Mosquitoes - on my arms, legs, everywhere

Nearing our tent, all of us realised there was something seriously amiss. It was unzipped, and the door flap hung open, revealing devastation inside. We stared.

"What on earth has happened here?" asked my father, peering into the tent, his military moustache bristling with indignation. "It looks like somebody has been searching for valuables."

We three kids gaped in wide-eyed wonder.

"Anything missing, do you think?" asked my sister.

"Not as far as I can see, but I think we should report it before we touch anything. The police will need to photograph the scene of the crime. Come along, we'll go and report it at the campsite office."

I tore my eyes from the mess inside. Darkness was falling, but I had seen that the little camp stove had toppled over, clothes and sleeping bags were strewn about, milk had been spilt, and plates and pans were scattered everywhere.

We trudged to the campsite office near the entrance gates. Shapes shuffled in the shadows under the trees, and I knew the ponies were watching us.

No lights burned in the campsite office and the door was locked.

"It's all closed up, now what?" asked my sister. "Wait, it says here: *Ring bell for attention out of hours or emergencies.*"

My father pressed the button firmly, and somewhere, a long way away, I heard an electric bell ring. As we waited, I stared at the flyers pasted on the windows of the office. *Brownsea Island Boat Ride, Tour Athelhampton House, Visit Poole Pottery, Visit Bournemouth Winter Gardens!*

I jumped in fright as something snickered a few feet away.

"Ponies," said my sister.

Human footsteps approached and an ancient figure stepped into view. An old man peered inquiringly at us, his scraggly white eyebrows raised in question.

"You rang?" he quavered.

"Good evening," said my father. "I'm here to report a robbery. Our tent has been broken into while we were away on a walk. I wonder if you could phone the police for us. I expect they'll want to come out and examine the crime scene."

"What was stolen?" asked the old man, "Are you missing any valuables?"

"Not that we can see yet," said my father, "but the thieves left a frightful mess."

"It was the ponies."

"Pardon?"

"The ponies broke into your tent, hehe," cackled the old man. "They do it all the time."

Something snorted in the darkness.

"I'm sorry, but it can't have been the ponies. The zip was undone."

"T'was the ponies! Clever little buggers! They've learnt to open tent zips with their teeth. And if they cain't git in that way, sometimes they'll just lean on a tent until it gives way. Betcha they've eaten all your food if you left it lying around in the tent. They ain't tidy neither, they always leave a helluva mess!"

We gaped at him. My father thanked him quickly and we hurried back to our tent.

The old man was right, of course. The ponies had unzipped our tent and helped themselves to our provisions, leaving a trail of destruction.

"Well, we've still got sausages," said my father cheerfully. "No bread rolls to put them in, but at least they left us something for supper."

He lit the little gas stove and we cooked, shared and ate the sausages that hadn't been trampled. They tasted good, but sausages on their own are not an exciting meal. And washing plates and a skillet in cold water isn't fun, either.

With just a single lantern to share between us, we had an early night. I wanted to read in bed, but the ponies had broken my flashlight so that was out of the question. As the ponies stamped and snuffled around our tent, I drifted off to sleep, but not for long.

Whispered voices woke me up. My brother was trying to attract my father's attention.

"Dad!"

"What?"

"I need the toilet!"

"What?"

"I need a wee."

"Can't it wait?"

"No."

"Well, go to the toilet block."

"What about the ponies?"

"They won't hurt you."

Silence.

"Well, just go round the back of the tent if you want."

"Okay."

Rustling. Buzz of the zipper. Footsteps round the tent. Splashing.

"What on earth do you think you're doing?" roared my father, fully awake now. "When I said go round the back of the tent, I didn't mean *on the back* of the tent!"

"Sorry."

I scratched a mosquito bite and drifted back to sleep, not at all sure if camping was really my thing.

The next day, breakfast was cancelled. The ponies had eaten the Kelloggs Rice Crispies and sugar, and kicked over the milk. They'd guzzled the bread destined for toast.

No, I thought to myself, *I don't think I really like camping.*

I imagine we were all quite relieved to pack up the tent, climb back into

Ivy and head for home.

Watercress, Olive and Lentil Pâté

Most of the UK's watercress comes from around the New Forest and that region, and it's a really healthy food packed full of vitamins. This recipe is a really quick and easy pâté that can be eaten straight away. If you prefer, pack it into a small loaf tin lined with transparent film, and allow it to set in the fridge overnight, ready for slicing the next day.

200g (7 oz) green lentils, washed then simmered for 20-25 mins in veg stock
100g (3½ oz) green olives
1 bunch watercress
Juice of half a lemon
Extra virgin olive oil
Sea salt and freshly ground black pepper

Method
- Place everything in a mixing bowl and blend with a hand-held blender or process in a food processor.
- Choose between smooth or chunky depending on how long you whiz it for.
- Season to taste and serve with fresh crusty bread.

❃ ❃ ❃

The days slipped by, and it was time to exchange the navy blue uniform of TH for the grey of Parkstone Grammar School for Girls on the outskirts of Poole. My sister was at the college in Bournemouth, and my brother was in boarding school. My parents didn't want me to attend the mixed grammar school in Swanage, and Wareham didn't have a grammar school.

Of course, this meant a long journey to and from school every day. I would have to walk to the station, catch a train to Poole, walk to Poole bus station, then catch a final bus to the school. However, because it was my first day, my mother decided, just this once, she would drive me.

Ivy bucked, stuttered and stammered her way to Poole. My mother's knuckles were white as she gripped the steering wheel, and mine were equally white as I hung onto my satchel. I was terrified, but not of my mother's driving. It was the thought of school that scared me. I knew that everybody else would have already made friends, and I was joining them in their second year.

"*Ach,* I'm not going to take you right into the school car park," announced my mother, "in case I have to reverse Ivy out. No, I'll just drop you at a bus stop if we see girls in Parkstone uniform."

That didn't take long. My mother stamped on Ivy's brake and we jolted to a stop. I shrank down in my seat as my mother jumped out.

"Is there somebody in the second year here?" she bellowed at the clusters of grey-clad girls.

I shrank down so low I could barely see over Ivy's dashboard. The girls swung round to stare first at my mother, then Ivy, then at me.

"Anyone in the second year who will look after a new girl?" repeated my mother.

I was mortified.

An extraordinarily pretty girl stepped forward, smiling. I wanted this whole nightmare to end as quickly as possible, so I grabbed my satchel and jumped out onto the pavement.

"Hello," smiled the girl. "I'll look after you. I'm Jo, what's your name?"

She was quietly-spoken, but exuded friendliness. Her huge brown eyes, with just a hint of naughtiness, smiled kindly at me. The other girls lost interest and turned away. My mother jumped back into Ivy and disappeared up the road in puffs of exhaust fumes.

I'm still grateful to Jo for rescuing me that bleak day. Without hesitation, she introduced me to Hilary and their circle of friends and I have much to thank her for. We stayed close friends all through school and still keep in touch. Today we are both grandmothers.

I believe my first form teacher was Miss Meniss, but a menace she wasn't. She was a giant of a woman, with hands like a bunch of bananas and feet the size of row boats, but there was nothing fierce about her. I believe she had been a novice in a convent, but had decided at the eleventh hour that she didn't want to be a nun after all, and became a teacher instead.

I didn't do particularly well at school. As usual, my head was in the clouds. I dropped Latin as soon as I could, and did the bare minimum required for every subject except English and Art, and German, which I obviously found quite easy.

My group of friends was not sporty at all. Without question, the subject I disliked most was Physical Education, and the PE teacher was terrifying.

"Move!" she bawled. "Go after the ball, don't just stand there!"

Which was worse, hockey in the freezing cold, or playing rounders in the summer? On the playing fields, the only skill Jo, Hilary, Sally and I perfected was making daisy chains and wearing them as necklaces and crowns. I detested the smell of the changing rooms, and I loathed the white Airtex shirts and chafing culottes we had to wear.

And as if netball, rounders or hockey practice wasn't bad enough, the lesson always ended with a shower. We didn't have individual cubicles, it was a long line of water jets we had to run through.

I was mortified, and tried everything to get out of both PE and the shower run. I was already painfully shy, and the thought of stripping off all my clothes in front of everyone was excruciating, particularly as I was slow to develop. I didn't want to reveal my flat chest to the world.

As each girl ran through the shower, her name was ticked off on the register. If it was your 'time of the month', you whispered the fact to the PE mistress, and you were excused from showering. Every lesson I'd claim it was my time of the month and all went well for a few weeks. Then the PE mistress noticed the row of P's next to my name, and a letter was sent back to my parents expressing concern and suggesting I might need a visit to the doctor.

I tried to explain why I lied. Both my father and mother frequently walked around the house and garden with no clothes on, so had no sympathy for me at all.

"*Ach,* we're all built the same!" said my mother.

But we're not! I screamed inside my head. *You should see Iris, she's got a HUGE bust, and so has everybody, and my chest is as flat as a board. I'm the only one who isn't wearing a bra yet!*

There was nothing else for it, the showers had to be sabotaged. We all hated the showers, and we plotted a way to stop them for ever.

I don't remember who thought of it, (was it Jo, Hilary, Sally or me?) and I don't remember who carried out the deed, although I think it may have been me... I stole the keys that turned the shower on, and I hurled them from the window of the train.

Of course, the PE mistress reported the loss to the headmistress. The crime was announced in assembly, with orders for the culprit to return them immediately. But the best news was that the keys took ages to replace, so for weeks we didn't have to run through the shower.

Result!

As my chest remained flat, I resolved to do something about that, too.

14
Bras and Other Agonies

It didn't matter how often I lifted my vest and shirt to examine my progress, nothing seemed to be happening. My chest remained as flat as a becalmed lake.

There were a few girls in my class who still weren't wearing bras, but I was the last of my group. I decided a little white lie might be in order.

My mother was washing up, which was a good time to catch her before she disappeared into the garden. I grabbed a drying-up towel, and took a deep breath.

"Um, the PE teacher took me aside. She says it's time I wore a bra," I said, drying a plate so thoroughly I nearly rubbed the pattern off.

My mother stopped and stared at me, her hands still in the suds.

"She did what? *Ach*, but your chest is completely flat!"

I winced.

"I know, but that's what she said..."

"Ridiculous! Well, I suppose we'll have to buy one."

Success!

My friends all lived in Poole and had masses of shops to choose from, but Wareham offered only one possibility. It wasn't a department store with a lingerie department. It was a general store with a cobwebby, bow-fronted window and a bell that clanged when you pushed the door open. If my memory serves me correctly, it was called Cullens and it sold a little bit of just about everything. There were sweets in jars, groceries, a Lyons Maid ice cream freezer, and gardening implements. Cullens also sold a few items of clothes, like aprons, old ladies' bloomers and babies' bibs.

That Saturday, my mother marched me into Cullens. As she pushed open the door, the bell clanged, announcing our entry.

"*Ach*, that ridiculous school has insisted that my daughter must wear a bra!" she declared to the whole shop.

I cringed, my face turning beetroot as all the customers in the shop swung round to stare at me and my chest.

"Do you sell very small bras?" asked my mother.

My face flamed anew.

"I believe we have a couple," said the middle-aged assistant. "Let me measure…"

In full view of everybody, she leaned over the counter and slipped a tape measure around me.

"Hmm… Yes, very broad back but nothing at all in front," she mused.

I wanted the wooden floorboards under my feet to slide apart and the floor to swallow me up.

"These newfangled teachers, what are they thinking of?" tutted the assistant to nobody in particular. "Now, let me see… Ah, yes."

She pulled down an ancient-looking brown box from a high shelf, and blew the dust off it. She lifted the lid and we gazed at the garment nestled in tissue paper.

"Yes," she said, drawing it out, "this should do."

The bra was hideous. It was stiff, plain white cotton, and the cups were the shape of ice cream cones, rather like Madonna's would be many years in the future. It wasn't a bit like my friends' bras, all lacy and wispy with tiny flowers sewn on.

"I think this one will fit," said the assistant.

"*Ach,* she'll have to try it on," said my mother.

What? This is a general store, it doesn't have a fitting room!

"Hmm…" said the lady, "come into the store room. There's no door but we can do it behind a pile of boxes."

Could this day get any worse?

Behind the pile of boxes, my mother and the lady assistant watched me pull my jumper and vest off, and fumble with the hook and eye of the ghastly garment. I was mortified by their close scrutiny. Being thirteen isn't easy at the best of times.

"Yes, that'll have to do," said my mother, poking one cup with her forefinger and leaving a dent. "She'll have to grow into it."

I looked down. I had some growing to do because the cups were completely empty.

"Would you like to keep it on, dear?" the assistant asked me.

"Yes, please," I answered, pulling on my vest and jumper as quickly as I could before somebody walked in.

Back at home, I mastered the art of the sock-fill. With careful moulding, I could stuff my bra with socks and become a 34A in minutes. I had to stay alert though, because if I moved about too much, one side was liable to drop out without warning.

My mother had an extremely low opinion of teachers and their requests. In Domestic Science, one term's assignment was to make a reversible tabard.

"What is it you are doing?" asked my mother.

"We're going to make this reversible tabard," I said, showing her a sketch. "We have to bring enough fabric for it. And a zip. And buttons."

"A what?"

"A reversible tabard."

"But what is this thing for?"

"Um... I don't know really."

"Ridiculous! I shall phone the school."

Which, of course, she did.

I didn't hear the interchange because I was at school, but it was very clear that my mother's opinions had been passed to Miss Chapman, my Domestic Science teacher. At the next sewing class, she singled me out. Her sharp nose was pink with indignation.

"Victoria, I believe your mother phoned the school?"

"Yes, Miss."

I was cringing already. I knew what my mother was like in full flow.

"Would you kindly tell your mother that this term's assignment is to make an extremely useful tabard."

"Yes, Miss."

"Please tell your mother that sewing the tabard will teach you all kinds of sewing-machine skills."

"Yes, Miss."

"And tell her you will be receiving *invaluable* guidance on how to put in a zip."

"Yes, Miss."

"And you will learn how to make buttonholes. All essential life skills."

"Yes, Miss. But, Miss, what is a tabard?"

"Oh, for pity's sake!" Miss Chapman's nose was growing pink again. "As I said, it's an *extremely* useful garment. You can wear it at the beach. And it's reversible, so you can choose which side to wear."

I relayed Miss Chapman's message back to my mother who snorted, clearly unimpressed. At the end of term, my tabard was finished and I wouldn't be seen dead in it. I never wore it, and as far as I know, my classmates didn't wear theirs either.

My mother was also very forthright when it came to Cookery. Unfortunately, Miss Chapman taught this subject too. Every week we were given a list of ingredients to bring for the following week.

"*Ach,* what's this nonsense?" she would ask, running her eye down the letter I'd handed her from school. "Kwitchy? What's Kwitchy Lorraine?"

"Quiche. Quiche Lorraine."

"Who eats this rubbish? I shall give you the ingredients for the pastry, but I'm not wasting perfectly good cheese and bacon."

At the end of the lesson, we all put our finished dishes out on display. All my friends' quiches looked and smelled wonderful, golden and delicious.

My pastry-only dish looked ridiculous.

Quiche Lorraine

For the pastry:
1¼ cups plain flour
½ tsp salt
8 tablespoons chilled unsalted butter, cut into small cubes
1 to 2 tablespoons of iced water
For the filling:
6 lean bacon slices
¾ cup cream, at room temperature
¾ cup milk, at room temperature
3 eggs, at room temperature
1 tablespoons of unsalted butter, melted
1 cup grated Gruyère or good Cheddar cheese
Salt and freshly ground black pepper, to taste
Cayenne pepper, to taste

Method

- Pastry: in a bowl, stir together the flour and salt. Add the butter and, using a pastry blender or your fingertips, work the ingredients together quickly until crumbly. Then, while quickly stirring and tossing with a fork, add the iced water a little at a time just until the dough begins to hold together. Gather into a ball, wrap in plastic wrap and refrigerate for 30 minutes.
- Position a rack in the lower third of an oven and preheat to 220°C/425°F
- On a lightly floured work surface, flatten the ball of dough into a disk. Dust it with flour and roll out into an 11-inch round. Fit carefully into a 9 or 10-inch tart pan, or a 9-inch glass pie dish. Prick the dough in several places with a fork and refrigerate for 10 minutes.
- Partially bake the pastry shell until it just begins to colour, 10 to 12 minutes. If the pastry puffs up during baking, prick again with a fork to release the steam. Remove from the oven and set aside. Reduce the oven temperature to 190°C/375°F/Gas Mark 5.
- To make the filling, fry the bacon until crisp and golden, 3 to 5 minutes. Transfer to paper towels to drain. When cool enough to handle, crumble into small bits. Scatter the crumbled bacon over the bottom of the pastry shell.
- In a bowl, combine the cream, milk, eggs and melted butter. Using a whisk or fork, beat until well blended. Stir in the cheese and season with salt, black pepper and cayenne pepper. Pour into the prepared pastry shell.
- Bake until the custard is set and the tip of a knife inserted into the center of the custard comes out clean, 25 to 30 minutes. Remove from the oven and let stand for several minutes before serving.

I dreaded Cookery. Miss Chapman only had to look at me for her nose to start turning pink, and my end of term grade was understandably poor. As soon as I could, I dropped Domestic Science like a red-hot platter.

Luckily, I learned everything I needed to know about cooking and sewing from Auntie Jean. If Miss Chapman had seen the things I produced at Annabel's house, I think she would have been surprised.

❀ ❀ ❀

School Report

English: Victoria is capable of producing good work. Unfortunately, she rarely does.

Mathematics: Victoria seems unable to grasp the fundamental principles.

Domestic Science: Victoria's work is extremely variable.

PE: I fear only a gargantuan effort will help Victoria improve.

❀ ❀ ❀

Oh, how happily I dropped Latin and Domestic Science! I would have dropped Physical Education and Maths too, had I been allowed, but there were education laws in place to stop me from doing that. I continued with Geography, even though we only ever seemed to learn about rubber farming and tea plantations. I longed to learn about countries like Spain, which even then held an attraction for me. How surprised would I have been if I'd known that my destiny was to live in a tiny Spanish mountain village one day?

I remember two Geography teachers. One was pleasant enough, but had the annoying habit of saying 'fair enough' dozens of times during a lesson. We used to keep a tally sheet, marking it off every time she said 'fair enough'. I think 32 was the record in one lesson.

The other Geography teacher was rather slovenly in appearance. Her black stockings often had holes or ladders, revealing unappetizing expanses of white flesh. She was hugely over-endowed, and would come into the classroom, sit at the teachers' desk and, accompanied with an audible sigh of relief, lift up her ample bosom to rest on the desk in front of her.

I didn't enjoy any subjects particularly, except English and Art.

I wasn't especially skilled in art, but I could draw and paint reasonably well. For me, art was a relaxation; while my hands sketched or painted, my head was in the clouds, weaving stories, and daydreaming.

Although English was much more disciplined, I loved it. Every new book was a stepping stone to a new world, and into other people's lives and adventures. In those days, 'Comprehension' exercises were popular. We had to read an excerpt from a book, then answer questions about it. I would read the excerpt, which could be from any classic like *Treasure Island*, *Black Beauty*, or *Nineteen Eighty-Four*. When it came to an end, I'd be annoyed. What happened next? So I'd take the book out of the library and read every spare moment I had.

Most adults can name at least one teacher they had in childhood who

103

inspired them. For me, it was our formidable English teacher, Mrs Hall. Nobody ever forgot to do the homework she set, or talked during her lessons. She had our absolute attention at all times, and we respected her. I know I have Mrs Hall to thank for learning the basics of English language, and stylistic devices.

Years later, I wondered what she would have thought had she known I would become an English teacher. And more recently, what would she have said if she'd known I became a writer? I think she'd have stared with disbelief, much as I still do now.

However, I don't think she would have been very impressed had she read my books. I think she would have whipped out her red pen and started crossing out and scribbling comments in the margin, right from page one.

I was at a bit of a disadvantage because I lived so far from my school. I didn't have any friends in Wareham because they went to other schools, so I never met anybody, except for Annabel, my friend and neighbour.

Annabel and her parents were not regular churchgoers, and neither was my family. Had I known about my mother's background, I would have understood why. The events behind that tale I shan't divulge now, it belongs in another *Old Fools* book.

I don't really know why Annabel decided to go to confirmation classes but I went along too. I'm ashamed to admit it was the thought of wearing a beautiful white dress that attracted me, not the meaning behind the ceremony.

I didn't mind the confirmation classes which were held at the vicarage. The vicar was a kind, fatherly man, easily embarrassed, who never tested to check if we had been listening. As he droned on about the Kingdom of Heaven, I disappeared inside my head, as usual. Auntie Jean helped us to choose white *broderie anglaise* fabric, then lay out patterns, and cut and sew our dresses.

The day of our confirmation arrived. I loved my dress and white shoes. We'd been told to bring posies of flowers, if we wanted, to hold when our photographs were taken before and after the ceremony. Auntie Jean had made ours, using flowers from her garden. She'd wound white satin ribbon round the stems, finishing it off with a bow, and the result was very pretty.

We were standing in the churchyard before the service as Auntie Jean took our photographs, when the vicar appeared, smiling and benevolent.

"That's a delightful posy of flowers you have there, Victoria," he smiled. "Are they scented?"

"Yes," I said.

The next few moments were unfortunate. Just as I helpfully held up my posy for him to sniff, the vicar bent down to smell it. The poor man's face was buried deep in my bunch of flowers.

"I'm terribly sorry," I said, horrified, as the vicar straightened hurriedly, a smudge of yellow pollen on the end of his nose.

"That's quite all right," he said, "it wasn't your fault...ah...ah...ahtishoo!"

He pulled out a large white handkerchief from somewhere in the folds of his surplice and blew his nose heartily.

But the damage was done.

Lady St Mary is a church of Anglo-Saxon origin, not far from Wareham quay on the river Frome. It is unusual as the church tower sports a fish, and being very large inside, every sound echoes. The visiting bishop, resplendent in his embroidered robes, conducted the confirmation service.

Lady St Mary Church, Wareham

"Heavenly Father, by the power of your Holy Spirit..."

"Ah...TISHOO!" came from the side of the church.

The bishop's eyebrows twitched but he ploughed on.

"Guide and strengthen us by the same Spirit..."

"Ah...TISHOO!"

It was like an explosion, the sound bouncing off the stone walls and the unique hexagonal lead font which dates back to the year 1200.

The poor vicar buried his red face in his handkerchief as the bishop's cold eyes lighted on him.

"Almighty and ever-living God, you have given these your servants..."

"Ah...TISHOO!"

And so the service continued, punctuated by the vicar's sneezes. And, sadly, I was the one to blame.

❈ ❈ ❈

"*Ach,* why don't you join Wareham Youth Club?" asked my mother, tired of hearing me complain that my friends lived so far away and I couldn't see them except at school.

I thought about it. Maybe that wasn't such a bad idea. After all, I might meet some *boys.*

Welsh Rarebit

Serves 4

25g (1 oz) butter
25g (1 oz) plain flour
150g (5 oz) mature grated Cheddar cheese
1 egg yolk
4 slices bread

Method

- Preheat the grill to high.
- Melt the butter in a non-stick saucepan and stir in the flour.
- Cook over a low heat for 30 seconds, stirring constantly.
- Simmer for 3 minutes, constantly stirring, until the sauce is thick and smooth.
- Add the cheese and egg yolk.
- Cook until the cheese melts, stirring constantly.
- Set aside to cool.
- Place the bread on a baking tray lined with aluminium foil and toast on each side until golden-brown.
- Spread the cheese sauce thickly over the bread, making sure the slices are completely covered so the edges don't burn.
- Return to the grill for 20 - 30 seconds longer until lightly browned and bubbling.
- Serve piping hot.

15
Youths and Cake

The Youth Club sessions were held in some kind of community hall in Wareham. I vaguely remember the hall being on the quay, behind black metal gates, beside The Quay Inn, but I may be wrong. My first visit was terrifying and taught me that I was different. I didn't speak like the other kids did. I had a posh public school accent and the other kids spoke with broad Dorset accents.

None were unkind to me or pointed out my strange way of speaking much beyond, "'Ere, why d'you talk funny?" but I wasn't comfortable, so I remained silent unless absolutely necessary.

Most of the Youth Club members were girls. They hung around in groups, talking about clothes and watching the few boys from the corners of their eyes. I didn't have many clothes, so I raided my sister's wardrobe, hoping I might fit in better if I paid more attention to fashion.

My sister was good at sewing and had loads of mini dresses hanging in her wardrobe. They didn't really fit me very well as I was still lacking in the bosom department, and I was taller and bigger-built than my sister, but that didn't stop me borrowing them, one by one. My sister also had quite a fetish for shoes. I tried them on and discovered they were too tight for me and pinched.

Did that stop me? No, of course not. I walked down to the Youth Club in dresses that were too tight, and shoes that gave me blisters, confident that the other girls would accept me now. I felt far more fashionable and walked a little taller. I was desperate to fit in.

Unfortunately, the raiding of my sister's wardrobe backfired somewhat. It sparked conversation, but, sadly, I was no closer to integrating.

"You live in one of them big houses, up beyond the almshouses, eh?" asked one girl.

"Er, yes…"

"Your parents rich then?"

"Er, no, not really, why?"

"Well, 'cos you talk funny, all posh like, an' you got so many clothes you wear sumfin diff'rent every day."

I persevered for a few months, and even developed a crush on a spotty youth called Barry, but I was never really happy at the Youth Club. Barry never noticed me, and when he started dating a tiny platinum blonde called

Janice Parry, I gave up. She had pierced ears and a skirt shorter than Twiggy's and I knew I was wasting my time.

My sister, being four years older, was beginning to date boys. She was a good tennis player, and like my mother before her, began to meet boys at the Tennis Club.

"*Ach,* bring your boyfriends back home to meet us any time," my mother told her.

It was summertime, and my mother spent most of her time in the garden and greenhouse, absorbed by seedlings, shrubs and propagation projects. My father did the digging, built small walls, erected fencing and took on any of the heavier jobs that needed doing.

Both my parents loved the sun, and they were both, unlike me, totally unselfconscious about their bodies. As soon as the sun came out, they threw off their clothes and carried on with their household and gardening chores completely naked. Our garden was big, and the fences and hedges were high, so nobody could see in.

I'm very glad I wasn't home the time it happened, but my sister told me all about it. She'd been playing tennis with a boyfriend, and when he dropped her off at our house, she'd invited him in.

"Come in and have a cold drink," she said. "and I'll introduce you to my parents."

He agreed, parked the car and the pair of them went inside.

"I'm home! Anybody in?" she called, but nobody answered.

Dumping her tennis racquet in a corner, my sister poured them each a lemonade.

"Where are your parents?" asked the young man.

"I don't know, probably outside working in the garden. We'll take them a lemonade."

They stepped out of the French doors into the garden. My sister looked around but could see neither of my parents. Then she caught the sound of hedge shears.

"Oh, I think my father's at the bottom, cutting the hedge," she said. "Follow me."

They found my father standing on a stepladder, clipping the hedge. Apart from shoes, he was completely starkers.

"Um, I've brought Peter to meet you," said my sister, "and here's some cold lemonade."

My father climbed down the steps and gravely shook hands with Peter.

"How do you do," he said.

"Nice to meet you, sir," said Peter, deadpan.

"Good game of tennis?"

"Oh, jolly good! We played doubles, and it was a very close game."

As Peter spoke, he looked neither left nor right, and certainly not down.

"Oh good, who did you play with?"

"James Graham and his cousin, Susan, do you know them?"

"I believe I do," said my father, sipping his lemonade. "Isn't that the Grahams from Stoborough? Let me see, Susan would be the oldest daughter?"

"Yes, Susan is the oldest, then there's Katherine, I think. Of course James has brothers and sisters, too. All members of the Tennis Club."

My sister, telling me all about this after the event, was chuckling.

"Both of them were pretending there was nothing abnormal about the situation at all," she said. "They were both being so *British!*"

I laughed like a drain at her description.

"And the really funny thing was, both of them were so determined to act as though there was nothing unusual, neither of them could find a way to finish the conversation. So they just kept on talking about the Tennis Club, weather, politics, everything!"

"Well," I said, "it's a good thing you didn't decide to introduce him to Mother too. I know she was planning to pull out all the seed trays from under the bench in the potting shed for sterilising. She didn't have a stitch on either, and she'd have probably been on all-fours when you and Peter went to find her."

We laughed until we had to hold our stomachs.

❊ ❊ ❊

In 1969, I was fourteen years old when two momentous things happened. Humans walked on the surface of the moon, and I got my first part-time job.

The teachers at school were very excited. Televisions (black and white, of course) were set up in various places in the school building and some of the teachers allowed us to watch. The moment was captured. Neil Armstrong stepped onto the lunar surface, and the world gasped.

"That's one small step for man, one giant leap for mankind," he said, and history was made.

Of course I was interested, but fourteen-year-olds are very self-obsessed, and I'm sure I was no different. Getting a job and making some money to pay for new loons was at the forefront of my mind. My mother thought loons, brightly-coloured hipster bell-bottom trousers, were hideous, but we loved them.

"*Ach,* you look like crazy carthorses," she said in disgust.

Later on, Levi or Wrangler jeans became the fashion. We would wear them so tight that we'd need to lie back on our beds and hook a coat-hanger in the zipper and pull hard to fasten them. And to ensure they were moulded exactly to our bodies, we sat wearing them in the bath. My mother rolled her eyes.

A vacancy for a chambermaid arose at a hotel on the outskirts of Wareham. I went for an interview knowing there were two applicants for the job. I was the second to arrive, just as the first applicant was finishing her interview.

"Thank you, Janice," said the hotel proprietor. "I'll let you know if you have been successful."

Janice looked at me just at the same moment as I looked at her. Our eyes locked in horror. It was Janice Parry from the Youth Club, my rival in love. She left and the hotel owner turned to me.

"Victoria? Come about the chambermaid job?"

"Yes."

"So, you're a student?" asked the proprietor, glancing at my application form.

"Yes, I'm still at school actually."

"But you're available to work on Saturdays and Sundays?"

"Oh, yes."

"What experience do you have with housework?"

"Um, I always tidy my room."

"Anything else?"

"I often clean the house." *Blatant lie.*

"And are you used to cleaning bathrooms?"

"Oh yes."

My fingers were crossed behind my back.

"Beds?"

"Yes, I make my bed..." Inspiration suddenly hit me. "Oh, and when I went to boarding school I learned how to make hospital corners."

I'm pretty sure it was the hospital corners that landed me the job.

So although Janice won spotty Barry, I won the job. I decided I had the much better deal and began to dream of the loons I would buy.

It was only a small hotel, but it catered for a steady stream of visitors who arrived to enjoy Dorset and its many attractions. Wareham is an attractive market town surrounded by Saxon walls and steeped in history. The walls still remain, encircling the original town, and it is possible to walk almost the entire circle.

Any tourist visiting Dorset, as well as enjoying more sunshine than most counties of England, will be spoilt for choice for places to visit. Castles, prehistoric remains, ancient monuments and hundreds of miles of spectacular coastline beckon.

Of course, Dorset, or Wessex as it was known in Medieval times, is Hardy country. Thanks to Mrs Hall's English lessons, I had a passion for Thomas Hardy's books and poetry. I had visited Hardy's cottage in Bockhampton, and Max Gate, his former home, many times. Hardy's hometown of Dorchester is called Casterbridge in his books, most famously in *The Mayor of Casterbridge*.

Plenty of tourists came to the hotel intent on viewing Hardy country, many of them American.

Max Gate, the former home of author Thomas Hardy,
located in Dorchester, Dorset, England.

One Saturday, the hotel proprietor handed me some keys.

"Morning, Vicky, could you start with Number 7 today, please? It's that American couple. They've already checked out, so it'll need a complete change."

I took the keys, gathered my cleaning products and made my way to Room 7, stopping on the way to pick up clean sheets and towels from the linen cupboard.

Inside Room 7, I stripped the bed and noticed that the occupants had left a book behind on the bedside table. I picked it up and read the title. *Hardy's Dorset,* I believe it was called.

Resisting the urge to flick through it, I cleaned the bathroom, then opened the mini-fridge. On a plate in the fridge sat perhaps two-thirds of a beautiful Dorset clotted cream chocolate cake.

I stared at it for a moment, and it stared back.

Well, Cake, the occupants of Number 7 have already gone, so I imagine it wouldn't matter if I just had a little taste of you?

As the cake didn't reply, I guessed it was giving me permission to eat it. I grabbed a knife, and took the plate with me over to the bed. I sat down, cut myself a sliver, and munched happily.

What do you think, Cake? It'd be okay to have another slice, wouldn't it?

No reply. Definitely no argument.

This time the slice of cake I cut was much more generous. I swung my feet up onto the bed and picked up the book from the bedside table. It looked interesting, so I leaned back on the pillows.

I was absorbed in the book and munching happily on the cake when the door handle turned.

Clotted Cream Chocolate Cake

Preparation: 20 minutes
Cooking: 1 hour
Makes about 10 slices

125g (4½ oz) butter, softened
175g (6 oz) light soft brown sugar
2 eggs
125g (4½ oz) self-raising flour
1 tsp baking powder
30g (1 oz) good quality cocoa powder
150g (5¼ oz) white chocolate
227g (8 oz) clotted cream
250g (8¾ oz) icing sugar

Method
- Preheat the oven to 180°C/350°F/Gas Mark 4. Lightly grease and base line an 18 cm (7 inch) loose-bottomed cake tin.
- Place the butter and brown sugar in a large bowl. Using a fork, mash together until they blend together into a paste.
- Add the eggs one at a time, whisking well after each.
- Add the flour, baking powder and cocoa.
- Stir through until you have a lovely dark cake mix. Roughly chop 100g (3½ oz) of the chocolate and add to the mixture along with 100g (3½ oz) of the clotted cream. Stir to combine and transfer to the prepared tin.
- Bake for an hour. It's a good idea to put some foil or a drip tray under in case of leaks during baking.

Icing
- Mix together the remaining clotted cream with the icing sugar and set aside.
- Remove the cake from the oven. Leave in the tin for about 15 minutes then tip out onto a cake rack.
- When completely cool, use a large knife to slice the cake in half horizontally.
- Fill the cake with a quarter of the icing then cover with the rest. Grate or curl the remaining chocolate and scatter over the cake.

16
Wales

I stared at the opening door in sheer horror. My mouth was full of clotted cream chocolate cake but my jaws had frozen, mid-chomp. The book fell into my lap.

In the doorway stood my boss, the hotel owner. Time stood still.

Oh no, Janice Parry is going to get this job after all.

He stopped, and his mouth dropped open when he saw what I was doing. I was supposed to be making up the bed with fresh linen, not leaning back on the pillows of a guest bed, reading a book, stuffing my face with chocolate cake.

But worse was to come. Behind him I could hear the American couple, Mr and Mrs Matthews, approaching.

I dropped the book, jumped off the bed and swallowed my mouthful of cake, all in one movement. My boss's face had turned an unhealthy shade of purple.

"I cannot believe…" he started, as Mrs Matthews popped her head round the door, then came in.

"Gee! I sure am glad you're eating that cake!" she said, eyeing the much-reduced cake on the plate. "We hoped somebody would eat it, didn't we, Chuck? Too good to waste and we couldn't take that on the airplane with us really."

My boss was still doing a codfish impression, but he closed his mouth, although his eyes were still bulging alarmingly.

"And y'all found our book on your Thomas Hardy!" chimed in Mr Matthews. "That's what we came back for. Wanted to show the folks back home where we'd been."

"Much obliged to y'all for cleaning our room and finding our book," said Mrs Matthews. "We've really enjoyed our stay in your quaint little hotel. Now we must hurry or we'll miss that airplane."

They bustled out, but not before Mr Matthews had stuffed a crisp £5 note into my uniform pocket.

My boss shook his head, stared at me for a moment, then hurried after them. Somehow I'd got away with it, and after I'd been scolded by my boss, the matter was never mentioned again. Janice Parry didn't get my job after all, but I'd learned my lesson.

❄ ❄ ❄

I wasn't very good at tennis, or any sport, but I always wanted to ride a horse. Even the criminal New Forest ponies hadn't put me off. I continued to plead but my parents wouldn't allow it, saying that it was far too expensive. Although I now had a job, I couldn't afford regular lessons. However, another opportunity to ride horses presented itself.

"Why don't you go on this Youth Hostel holiday?" asked my mother, waving a newspaper advertisement in my direction.

"You know I didn't like the Youth Club much."

"*Ach,* this is completely different, nothing to do with a Youth Club. Youth Hostels are a way of staying in wonderful places in England and Wales. You can stay in a castle, or mansion, or farm, all very cheap!"

My mother liked to save money.

"I don't think…"

"Read it! It's a pony trekking holiday in Wales."

"Oh!"

I read the details and decided it did look rather appealing.

"Now that you have your new job, you can save up and go if you want. Your father and I will help."

I mentioned it to Annabel, and she rather liked the idea too. Auntie Jean and Uncle Frank had no objections, so we both booked.

The description ran something like this: *Enjoy six days riding our native Welsh cobs and ponies on treks across the picturesque Black Mountains. Enjoy the Brecon Beacons with its wonderful views, interesting riding trails and mountain streams. We cater for riders of all abilities.*

We would be staying at one particular Youth Hostel in the Brecon Beacons national park. On one of the days, we'd trek to another Youth Hostel and stay there the night. It sounded perfect.

Annabel and I spent ages planning and deciding what we needed to pack. It was summertime, but good weather can never be relied upon in Britain. Therefore, rain-proof jackets and wellington boots were essential, as were jeans, T-shirts and sweaters. Then came the question of underwear.

"I think I've had a brilliant idea," I said. "Rather than taking lots of pairs of knickers, or less and then having to think about washing and drying them, why not take paper pants?"

"Paper knickers?"

"Yes, I saw them at Boots the Chemist. They come in packs. I'm going to buy a couple of packs, I think! They're disposable so I won't have to worry about washing and drying them, I'll just throw them away at the end of the day."

Genius.

Annabel didn't follow my lead, which was probably very wise.

Our holiday took place about 45 years ago, so I'm a little fuzzy over exactly where we stayed in the Black Mountains. I believe we slept in a 'bunkhouse' and I remember that there was a roster sharing out the chores. Some cooked, others cleared up after the meal. Those not working were free to sit on beanbags and sing *Where have all the flowers gone?* while one of our fellow guests, a German with long hair, strummed his guitar.

When we arrived, all our mounts were tethered in a line outside in the yard and we were allocated a pony each. Annabel was given Dougal, and my mount and companion for the week was a sturdy little mare with calm, liquid eyes and a shaggy mane. Her name was Megan. She sized me up briefly then carried on munching hay from the rack on the wall.

We were handed a bundle of reins, rugs, brushes, hoof-picks, saddles, and additional horsey paraphernalia, all baffling to a novice like me.

Annabel and Dougal

First we had to put a halter on our ponies, then take it off again. Megan didn't mind that, so long as I didn't get in the way of her hay munching.

"Good," said Jack, our trek leader. "Now you will groom your ponies. Give your pony a good brushing down."

I enjoyed that, and I think Megan did too, although she didn't stop munching long enough to tell me.

Megan and me

"Now," said Jack, "pick out each foot with your hoof pick. Avoid the frog and the quick, and as you groom, check the horse for lumps, bumps or swellings."

Obediently, we did as asked. Megan didn't seem to mind standing on three legs while I picked her hooves. It certainly didn't spoil her appetite.

"Is your pony still munching?" I asked Annabel, beside me. "Mine never seems to stop."

"No, he stopped ages ago."

"Right," said Jack, "now for the bridles. Put the reins over your pony's head, like this."

Done.

"Put the bit in the horse's mouth."

For the first time, Megan objected, and I knew why. I was interfering with her food intake.

"Put a finger on each side of the bit and gently push against the horse's mouth," said Jack.

"Ouch!"

I think Megan mistook my novice fingers for a bunch of carrots.

"Victoria, it's a good idea to put your thumbs in the very corner of Megan's mouth, where she has no teeth."

Now he tells me!

We succeeded in the end, after much fumbling. By now, Megan had finished her own hay and had started on Dougal's.

"Well done, everyone," said Jack, as I rubbed my bruised fingers. "And now for saddling up."

We all watched as Jack demonstrated with his pony.

"Put on the blanket first. Place the front on the horse's withers, and slide it down a bit so the hair isn't pushed into an unnatural position. Place the saddle gently on the horse's back and buckle up the girth."

That looked simple enough. I followed his instructions and as Megan munched, I slipped the girth around her sturdy middle and buckled it quite tightly, allowing space for just two (bruised) fingers, exactly like Jack showed us.

"And now it's time to mount! Stand next to your pony's left front leg."

We did so.

"Hold the reins in your left hand. Put your left foot in the stirrup. Stand on your left foot and swing your right leg over ... and there we are!"

Jack was astride his mount, and our party began to copy his movements.

"I did it!" called Annabel, patting her Dougal's neck.

Megan stood munching quietly as I positioned myself correctly. I placed my foot in the stirrup and swung myself up. The next thing I knew, I had landed with a thud on my backside on the ground on the other side of Megan. The entire saddle had rotated; the girth was much too loose. Megan probably rolled her eyes but she didn't even stop chewing.

How can that be? I had tested the girth. I'd left space for just two fingers.

"Ah, Victoria," said Jack who had appeared at my elbow. "My fault, I should have warned you about our Megan. She's a bit of a devil, plays that trick on all her new riders."

"Well, she got me good and proper!" I said, still rubbing my sore bottom. "How does she do it?"

"She's a crafty one! She inhales as you buckle up her girth, so of course it's much too loose. Next time, wait for her to exhale before you buckle it."

We hadn't been on a single trek yet, and I already had bruised fingers and a bruised behind.

The next morning, we saddled up with no mishaps. Megan had finished her breakfast and was contentedly cropping grass as I prepared her. I was extra careful with her girth, and the saddle fitted with no problems. I was one of the first to mount.

If you are an experienced horse rider, pony trekking is probably not for you. The pace is leisurely as the ponies follow each other, nose to tail. There is plenty of time to enjoy the view as the ponies plod along. It suited me just fine.

One of our party was a tall German who had come with his companion, the chap who played the guitar in the hostel every evening. The pair were friends but had very different personalities. The guitar player was a free spirit, quietly-spoken with long hair and a leather band around his forehead. His tall friend was loud and demanding.

"Jack! We make our horses run here, *ja?*" he shouted to our trek leader.

"No, Klaus, we don't."

To be honest, Klaus, the tall German, looked a little ridiculous astride his pony. His legs were so long, his feet nearly touched the ground. But this didn't stop him urging his mount to go faster. He would sneakily hold his pony back so that he could urge it into a canter to catch up with the party. Klaus's pony was obedient, but refused to go faster than a slow jolting trot, which meant that Jack quickly saw what he was up to.

"Klaus! Our ponies aren't built for speed! And this terrain is dangerous. A pony could easily end up with a hoof in a rabbit hole and a broken leg."

He waited for Klaus to catch up, and kept his eye on him from that moment. Klaus sulked but never managed to turn his pony into a racehorse.

Megan, my pony, was definitely not built for speed. Actually, she wasn't really built for any kind of movement at all. Her mind was only occupied with filling her stomach. Persuading her to abandon a tasty clump of grass and resume our journey was often extremely difficult.

By the end of the first day in the saddle, I was loving it, but I was sore. Muscles that I didn't even know existed ached and throbbed.

And I discovered that my decision to pack only paper knickers was probably not a very clever idea after all. When I undressed that night, I was shocked.

"Annabel?"

"Yes?"

"You know those paper knickers I brought?"

"Yes?"

"Well, I wore them today."

"And?"

"Well, they've gone."

"What do you mean, gone? Stolen?"

"No, gone."

All that was left was a band of elastic round my hips and another round each leg, with a few tattered pieces of paper hanging off. The rest of my paper knickers had simply worn away.

❋ ❋ ❋

The pony trekking holiday was soon over, and I was back home in Wareham. It was hard persuading my mother to take us out. Unless there was some kind of horticultural attraction, she preferred to stay at home pottering in the garden.

However, I do remember one family outing that didn't turn out quite as planned.

17
Fords

Dorset is a beautiful county, sprinkled liberally with picture postcard villages. Thatched cottages cluster around village greens. Dorset has more than its fair share of heathland, beaches, agricultural land and woodlands.

Once a year, we all climbed into Ivy the Land Rover for a springtime outing. Ivy was now a very old lady; she'd been elderly when my parents first bought her. However, she was happy to trundle along the country roads with us kids in the back and my mother gripping the steering wheel as though it was threatening to escape. Ivy chugged a little going uphill, and her engine was so loud we had to yell or use hand-signals, but she never let us down.

Except once.

In spring, shy, yellow primroses blossom on banks, and bluebells are a swathe of colour in the woodlands. No matter how many times I saw them, they took my breath away. As far as the eye could see, the blue flowers carpeted the ground, the flower-heads nodding in the soft spring breeze.

In those days, it wasn't illegal to pick wildflowers, and my mother dug up dozens to transplant into our garden. We gathered armfuls to put in every container we could find at home. I'm ashamed now that we picked so many, as wildflowers soon die when they are picked. We should have left them for other people and the wildlife to enjoy.

This particular time, we drove along a back country road where the trees overhead met to form a green tunnel. A little further ahead, the road forded a stream. My mother pushed her face near the windscreen, and stared ahead.

"What's the matter?" asked my sister.

"*Ach!*" said my mother, stamping on Ivy's brakes and sending us all flying in the back. "I don't know how deep this ford is. We've had a lot of rain recently."

"It looks quite deep," said my sister. "The water is flowing quite fast."

My mother stared at the water. We were still some distance away.

"Perhaps we should turn back?" somebody suggested. "Find another way?"

The road was deserted and she could have easily executed a three-point-turn, but my mother flatly refused.

"You *know* I don't reverse."

She opened Ivy's door and strode to the water's edge, thinking. She looked up and down the stream, then returned.

"*Ach,* I think it'll be okay," she announced. "I think Ivy is high enough to clear it. I'm going to take a run at it and go through as fast as I can."

Determinedly, she climbed back into Ivy and revved the engine like a racing driver.

"Hold tight!" she yelled and stamped on the accelerator.

Ivy careered bravely towards the water and straight through, her speed causing much splashing. Out of the other side she came and began to climb the slope.

"Well done, Ivy!" shouted my mother.

"Hooray!" we kids yelled in the back.

But our victory crow was premature. Without warning, the engine died.

"Quick!" yelled my sister. "We're rolling back into the water!"

My mother stamped on the brake and applied the handbrake.

"I *don't* reverse!" she muttered.

And there we sat, with water draining out of the engine and running off Ivy's paintwork in little rivulets, until eventually another car came along.

The car approached from behind. It wasn't a high car, in fact it was much lower than Ivy. But it had no problem fording the stream and overtaking us, then coming to a standstill in front of Ivy.

"Everything okay?" asked the driver, climbing out of his car. "Need any help?"

"*Ach,* thank you very much," said my mother. "We drove through the ford without a problem, and then the engine just stopped."

The man looked at the water still dripping off Ivy and making puddles on the road.

"Did you drive very slowly through the water?" he asked. "It's deep at the moment. If you drive through slowly, like I did, you will keep the engine dry."

"No," admitted my mother, "I drove as fast as I could."

"She drove like a bat out of hell," whispered my brother, making us snigger in the back.

"Well," said our advisor, "I'm afraid that's what's happened; your engine is soaked. Everything, including your spark plugs, got wet."

"So what do we do?"

"Nothing. You'll just have to wait until it all dries out, then she'll start up nicely again."

With a cheery wave he climbed back into his car and drove off, leaving us stranded. My mother propped up Ivy's bonnet, "to let the air blow through," and dabbed parts of the engine nervously with her headscarf. Obviously she wouldn't have recognised a spark plug even if it had bitten her on the end of her nose. We amused ourselves by racing sticks down the stream, and eventually, the engine dried.

My mother turned the key in the ignition and Ivy burst into life.

"Hooray!" we shouted, and clambered back in.

"Quick! Before Ivy stops again!"

Off we bucked and chugged and reached the bluebell woods without further mishap. We returned home via another route.

Back home, we filled the house with glorious bluebells until the air was heavy with their perfume. When we ran out of vases, we used jugs and milk bottles.

My father arrived home and we told him all about our day.

"Didn't you check how deep it was?" he asked my mother.

"Well, I got out of the car and looked at the water."

"So what made you decide to drive through?"

"*Ach*, don't be silly, you *know* I never reverse. And anyway..."

"Yes?"

"The water only came halfway up some ducks."

A second's silence, then we all roared with laughter.

To this day, I'm not convinced whether she was serious or not.

❁　❁　❁

I still had my chamber-maiding job and had managed to work just hard enough to keep it out of Janice Parry's clutches. My boss then asked me if I'd like to take on a little waitressing now and then, particularly at wedding functions. I happily agreed, although being rather shy and clumsy, I wouldn't be the best of waitresses.

Around that time, another girl from my school moved into Wareham. As we travelled every day on the train to Poole together, we became friends, although she was younger than I.

Marion Ford was a policeman's daughter and a bit 'fast' as Auntie Jean might say. We all wore mini skirts, but Marion's were micro minis. We all wore loons and platform shoes, but Marion's loons were slung lower on the hips, and her platform shoes were higher.

Marion taught me a lot. She talked about boys incessantly and I listened with wide eyes. She showed me how to turn the waistband of my school skirt over and over to make it shorter. She showed me how to hide my sensible school shoes in a bush and change them for much more unsuitable, strappy shoes, changing back before I got home. She showed me how to apply thick pancake make-up to my face and neck, and blend three colours of purple eyeshadow. She taught me how to moisten a cake of mascara and apply it with a brush.

"And look, here's how you curl your eyelashes. Take the curlers, grab the eyelashes and squeeze hard. Like this… See?"

She admired the result in her omnipresent little round magnifying mirror.

"And now for the false eyelashes. A line of glue, then stick, and press."

I wasn't a willing student. I found the strappy shoes uncomfortable, and applying the make-up was a pain, and it turned my towel orange when I washed it off. Marion's eyes were made up like Twiggy's, with black outlines, but I never mastered that. Neither did I master the false eyelashes, though I tried. How could girls wear them? They were so uncomfortable.

"Do you know anybody who might like to work a few hours waitressing?" asked my boss. "We've got a big wedding coming up and we could use an extra pair of hands."

I racked my brain, desperate to come up with somebody before my boss contacted Janice Parry.

"Um, I have a friend called Marion Ford," I said reluctantly. "I could ask her."

I wasn't sure how Marion would fit in really, with her pancake make-up and fluttering false eyelashes.

"Ah, is she the policeman's daughter? Yes, I know her father. If she wants the job, bring her along with you a bit early."

I asked Marion, and as she was keen, we both turned up on the afternoon of the function.

My boss looked at Marion as I introduced them, and I saw his eyebrows twitch. He showed her the kitchen, and explained how we worked, how the top table would be served first, and who would look after which area of the dining room.

"Well, that seems straightforward enough," she said.

"Right," said my boss. "Here is your uniform and this is your apron. Please go and change and report back to me. We don't have much time. Oh, and could you please remove some of your make-up. It's a little heavy for our establishment…"

Marion looked affronted, but accepted the uniform.

"I'm not taking it all off," she said to me as we changed. "I'll wipe some of me eyeliner and eyeshadow off, but I'm not taking off me false eyelashes for anybody."

Marion's false eyelashes were so thick and sweeping they almost created a breeze every time she blinked.

The wedding party and guests had arrived and were already seated.

"Good," said my boss as he looked us up and down at the inspection. "You both look tidy and presentable. Just one thing, Marion, take off the eyelashes, please."

Marion opened her mouth to argue, then thought better of it. She pouted and turned on her heel to head for the restroom.

"Time to get serving!" called Dawn, the head waitress, picking up her tray of starters. "Victoria, Marion, are you ready?"

"Yes, Dawn," I said and picked up my tray. "Marion, you don't have time to go to the restroom," I hissed.

"Yes, Dawn," echoed Marion, quickly tearing off the false eyelashes and throwing them aside. She grabbed her tray and followed me through the swing doors into the dining room.

It was a lovely wedding. Sunshine streamed through the big windows and onto the top table. In the middle sat the groom, handsome in his grey three-piece suit. The bride glowed, and the bride's and groom's parents beamed proudly. The tablecloths were crisp and white, decorated with a centrepiece of blue violets and snowy gypsophila, or baby's breath.

Soft music played in the background and the guests seemed to be enjoying their prawn cocktail starter. I made my way back to the kitchen when a little gesture caught my eye.

At the very end of the top table sat an ancient lady. Looking at her, I guessed she must be the bride's grandmother. The old lady caught my eye and quietly beckoned me over.

I stood at her side, smiling, but she beckoned me closer. I leaned over, straining to hear what she was saying, and caught that distinctive old-lady smell of lavender.

Prawn Cocktail

Serves 4

4 tbsp mayonnaise
2 tsp tomato ketchup
1 tsp tomato purée
A dash of Tabasco sauce
1 tsp salad cream
1 tsp lemon juice
Little Gem lettuce leaves, shredded
75g (2½ oz) very small cherry tomatoes, halved
500g (17½ oz) cooked prawns
A pinch of paprika, for garnish

Method
- In a bowl, mix the mayonnaise, ketchup, tomato purée, Tabasco sauce, salad cream and lemon juice.
- Mix the shredded lettuce leaves with the cherry tomatoes.
- Divide the salad mixture equally between 4 glass bowls.
- Keeping 4 garnish prawns aside, mix the prawns with the sauce.
- Spoon the prawn cocktail mixture over the salad in each glass bowl.
- Arrange a garnish prawn on each.
- Sprinkle with a pinch of paprika and serve immediately.

"I don't want to make a fuss, dear, and I know it's not your fault."

"Excuse me?"

"It's that time of year, of course," she said.

"I'm sorry?" I was baffled.

125

"I wouldn't have mentioned it, but it's just so big!"

"I'm sorry?" I was so close now that I could see the fine down on her papery cheek.

The old lady lifted a bony finger and pointed at her prawn cocktail.

"I wonder if you could possibly take it back to the kitchen and get me another? That insect looks as though he's there to stay. I tried to shush him away but he hasn't moved at all since I noticed him. Actually..." she leaned even closer, "I think he may be dead."

I followed her gaze and saw to my horror what she was looking at. Perched atop the green shredded lettuce and pink mayonnaise of the prawn cocktail, was a very large insect with numerous legs.

Except it wasn't an insect.

"I'm terribly sorry," I breathed as I whipped the prawn cocktail away. "I'll bring you another immediately."

Unfortunately, my eagle-eyed boss was lurking just inside the kitchen.

"What's that?" he asked. "Has somebody sent their food back?"

"Um..."

Too late. My boss was already peering closely at the offending dish. With great precision, he picked out the 'insect' with his finger and thumb and held it aloft.

"How," he said heavily, "just *how* did one of Marion's false eyelashes end up in a guest's prawn cocktail?"

It wasn't my place to say, so I grabbed a replacement prawn cocktail and sped it out to the old lady.

"I'm so sorry," I said again.

"Oh, don't worry!" she whispered. "I expect it just flew in. It's our little secret."

I didn't tell the nice old lady the truth. And my boss didn't require Marion's assistance at any more weddings. I just hoped that if he found himself short-handed, he wouldn't consider employing Janice Parry.

❀ ❀ ❀

My sister had been accepted to Exeter University, where she thrived. My wardrobe diminished because she took all her clothes with her. My brother was still at boarding school, so I was the only one at home.

I was supposed to be studying hard for my 'O' Levels but actually I was doing very little studying. I either had my head in a book, or in the clouds, daydreaming.

18
Money and Work

If only we could see into the future. At school, I was so quick to drop French and Latin, and I never even considered taking up Spanish, although I was given the opportunity. If only I'd known that in the future nearly all my friends and neighbours would be Spanish and I would be living in a Spanish village. Had I been offered a peep into what lay ahead, my school decisions wouldn't have been so hasty.

Instead of languages, I decided to take up Greek Mythology. A fascinating subject with wonderful stories, but, dare I say it, not really terribly useful?

I had to persevere with Maths, although there was very little point. Numbers confused me and still do. I could manage stuff like Venn diagrams because it was a picture, and even equations were kind of logical, but simple and compound interest defeated me. And questions like: *If a man can dig a four foot hole in two and a half hours, how long will it take eight men to dig a ten foot hole?* left me bewildered.

My Maths teacher, Miss Crowe, had given up on me a long time ago.

"Victoria! You're day-dreaming again! Get this question wrong and I'll sssssstring you up by the heelssss."

When it came to the mock exams, I failed miserably. Taking the same paper again, my result was even worse the second time, even though the questions were the same. The school decided that I shouldn't take Maths 'O' Level and I heartily agreed.

It was 1971, an exciting time. The Range Rover had been introduced, making Ivy the Land Rover look like something from a museum. We saw the first electronic calculators, massive things with blinking LEDs. Hot pants appeared, shocking the older generation. And Great Britain was preparing to make a monumental change.

Back in 1824, Lord Wrottesley proposed an utterly crazy idea in parliament. He suggested that Britain's currency should be decimalised. Such a foolish notion was roundly rejected, of course. What? Lose the guinea, shilling, half-crown, sixpence, ha'penny and florin? Unthinkable!

But now, more than one hundred and forty years later, Britain was on the verge of doing exactly that.

At first, three new coins were introduced into the old system: the 5p, 10p and 50p coins. That meant that on Decimal Day (or 'D Day'), the general public had already learned three of the six new coins.

Banks were closed on Wednesday, 10th February, until the morning of Monday 15 February, to enable everything in the clearing system to be processed. Customers' accounts were converted from pounds, shillings and pence, to decimal. These conversions were carried out manually, as most bank branches were not yet computerised.

Then, on February 15th, 1971, it all happened. I remember it was quite a smooth process as the government had done a good job of educating us before the day, and prices in shops were displayed in both new and old prices for a long time before and after 'D Day'.

However, some of the old folk complained bitterly, and I even overheard my mother asking my father, "*Ach,* yes, but how much is that in *real money?*"

A menu showing both prices

We sat our exams in the heat of summer, sitting in long rows in the school hall, teachers pacing up and down to check that nobody cheated. Our pens and pencils were in transparent plastic bags, and if we dropped something, or we wanted anything, we had to raise our hands.

"How did you do?" we asked each other afterwards. "Could you do number 3? It was impossible!"

It was a long wait for the results, and I wasn't looking forward to receiving them at all. Meanwhile, we were all going on Work Experience.

I'd given my future career some thought, and had accepted the fact that I would never be a vet. I wasn't really smart enough, and anyway, I had dropped all my science subjects. I thought becoming a zoo keeper was probably a bit fanciful, and again, I had no science or biology training. An artist or writer? Nowhere near talented enough. So what was left?

I decided that teaching would suit me very well. After all, to steal George Bernard Shaw's words, "Those who can, do; those who can't, teach."

That meant I needed 'A' Levels to get into a Teacher Training College, as they were called then. But first, I could go on a week's work experience in a school to see what it was all about.

What should I wear? I wanted to look fresh and businesslike so I opted for a white blouse and grey skirt.

I was sent to help in a reception class. As I watched the teacher welcoming each four-year-old and taking instructions from the parents, I felt completely out of my depth.

"Please make sure Susan drinks her milk today."

"Can you check that Johnnie doesn't pick his plaster off?"

"Maria has an odd pair of plimsolls in her PE bag. Does Scott have one of hers?"

"Colin's really worried about the letter 'A'."

"Please don't let Mark eat any cheese, it makes him sneeze."

How could she possibly remember all that *and* spend a day teaching? Wanting to be a teacher was madness! There must be less stressful careers.

A tiny warm hand slid into mine. I looked down. An earnest little face framed by light brown curls gazed up at me.

"Hello, what's your name?"

"Hello, I'm Vicky," I said. "I've come to help your teacher this week. And who are you?"

"I'm a kangawoo today. You can be a kangawoo too if you like. Why do kangawoos bounce?"

And I was hooked. Yes, I wanted to be a teacher, however hard that was going to be.

The morning flew past in a flurry of songs and activities. Not a second went by when I wasn't busy doing something, whether it was taking a child to the toilet or packing up crayons. I soon wished I'd worn flat shoes, and chosen to wear trousers instead of a skirt.

I had an hour for lunch and my friend, Iris, and I met. She was doing her work experience in another class in the same school. Our plan was to go to a local cafe to get something to eat. There was a small, greasy-looking cafe round the corner, so we sat down and ordered.

Both of us were talking nonstop about our morning as the food arrived.

"A little boy in my class disappeared," said Iris, picking up the tomato ketchup dispenser, a red plastic squeezy fake tomato.

"Did you find him?"

"Yep, we were all looking for him—this tomato sauce isn't coming out—and it turned out he'd climbed into the old newspapers cupboard and gone to sleep."

She laughed and gave the plastic tomato a hearty squeeze with her thumbs. It must have been blocked by a plug of congealed sauce, because the ketchup suddenly shot out in a hard, red jet.

I gasped as it hit me full in the face at pointblank range. It momentarily blinded me in one eye and dripped down my face, off my chin and down my white blouse. I was speechless. It was so awful that we both started laughing uncontrollably as we used a mountain of paper serviettes to try to clean me up. It was no use, of course.

I ran to the Ladies Room but the damage had been done. No amount of dabbing with water was going to improve matters much. I gave up with my white blouse but rinsed my face. I looked in the mirror, and a squinty, bloodshot eye stared back at me. Tomato ketchup has spices and vinegar as ingredients, and my eye was red and smarting.

The teacher blinked as she looked me up and down when I returned to the classroom.

"Whatever happened to you?" she asked. "You look as though you were caught in the crossfire of a gunfight at the OK Corral."

I loved my week of work experience and it cemented my decision of what I wanted to do after I left school. I would train to be a teacher. My friends also had interesting experiences at their respective placements, but for some, their experiences put them off pursuing a particular career.

My classmate Sue had always wanted to be a vet and was delighted that she would be helping in a local veterinary practice for a week. Her family's home was full of animals, and she was sure that training to be a vet was her future.

"So what happened?" I asked.

"Well, the first day was okay... I helped behind the reception desk answering the phone and booking appointments and stuff."

"And then?"

"Well, the vet said I should watch a routine dog castration."

"Oh! Yuk!"

"I know! Anyway, he asked me to stand at the business end of the operating table so I could see everything that was happening. It was a big dog they were doing, a boxer. They anesthetised it and laid it on its back, legs akimbo. Then they covered it all up with a sheet except for a square where its, erm, bits poked through."

Sue shuddered at the memory and I pulled a face in sympathy.

"So then the vet started operating, and I didn't want to watch him slice, so I stared hard at the bit of sheet next to what was going on. I didn't actually look at what the vet was doing at all."

"So did you get away with that?"

"Nope! There was a kind of splat, and the vet said, 'Get that for me, Susan.'"

"Oh no! What was it?"

"One testicle had kind of shot out and went skidding across the floor. I didn't have any choice, I had to get a tissue and pick it up."

That was the end of Sue's dream to become a veterinarian. I heard from her many years later, and she was then a very successful stockbroker working for an investment bank in London. Go figure.

❋ ❋ ❋

Next came the agony of opening the long brown envelope that arrived in the mail, containing examination results. I couldn't bring myself to open it, but let my mother do it as I sat on the stairs hugging my knees.

"*Ach,* they're not too bad," she said. "You have seven 'O' Levels, all A, B or C. You failed Geography. Never mind, you have enough to continue with 'A' Levels."

Well, that was a relief!

I know I should have been thinking about studying, but I was beginning to follow in Marion Ford's footsteps. No, I didn't plaster on make-up and false eyelashes, but my mind was often occupied by the subject of *boys.*

19
The Animal Sanctuary

I lost myself in day-dreams so romantic and unlikely I should have written them down and turned them into fanciful novels. I imagined I was going to meet my Prince Charming everywhere. Perhaps he'd be a guest at the hotel where I was a chambermaid? Or perhaps I'd bump into him on the train to school?

When neither of those things happened, I decided I needed to widen my circle of places I frequented. Wareham couldn't offer much. I didn't want to go back to the Youth Club, but I could go to the cinema. It wasn't big, in fact, the Rex's claim was that it was the smallest cinema in the south of England.

Of course I never met my Prince Charming there, but I did see some movies that I still recall today. I saw *Cat Balou, Seven Brides for Seven Brothers, Finian's Rainbow, Half a Sixpence, The Love Bug* and the Beatles' films. I usually went on my own or with Annabel.

I don't remember my parents ever going to the cinema, except on one particular occasion a few years before, when the whole family went. The film was *The Sound of Music* with Julie Andrews. I couldn't understand why we were going to see it, as it was so out of character for my mother and father to go to 'the flicks'. I also couldn't understand why my mother had a strange expression on her face throughout, and why she was so quiet afterwards.

As I write this, nearly 50 years later, I understand why the movie must have been so painful for her to watch. I have told the story in *Two Old Fools in Spain Again*.

How clearly I remember trips to the Rex cinema in West Street! The performance always began with the gaslights dimming, then the red velvet curtains swishing apart, revealing a silver screen. First we watched a 'B' movie and advertisements, then the gaslights were turned up again and ice creams were sold.

Back in the 1960s, I once saw a little mouse by my feet, sitting up and nibbling a piece of popcorn it was holding in its front paws. Annabel and I affectionately called the cinema 'the fleapit', even though it was a place we loved to go.

When the gaslights dimmed again, my heart pounded with excitement. Now the real performance was beginning! Above our heads, cigarette smoke swirled in the rectangular stream of light from the projectionist's room at the back, and music filled the hall. It was beginning!

I'm delighted to see from research on the Internet that the Rex never became a bingo hall as so many other cinemas were doomed to become. It is still going strong and has a website of its own. It is a little cinema with a long history and masses of character, beloved by locals.

I have to confess that it was at the Rex that I viewed my first 'naughty' movie. The film was certified as an '18' so I had to dress up and try to look older. To my relief they didn't question my age. I sat with huge eyes and watched Jane Fonda strutting her stuff in *Barbarella*.

In an attempt to broaden my horizons, and maybe meet my Prince Charming, I decided to look for another part-time job. Making beds and cleaning bathrooms was not really my idea of fun, and I was tired of being a chambermaid.

"I'm sorry," I told my boss, "I'm handing in my notice."

"Well, I'm sorry to hear that too, are you quite sure? I do have a list of girls who will jump at the chance of a job here."

"Yes, I'm sure."

Give it to Janice Parry, I don't care.

I was lucky, something perfect *did* turn up. It was a job that, though lowly paid, I would adore and keep until I left home two years later. I became a helper at an animal sanctuary in the depths of leafy Dorset.

And I loved it.

A little mini-bus collected me and the other workers early in the morning. We trundled up hill and down dale until we arrived at the gates of the sanctuary. Dogs barked as we drove in, and ponies lifted their heads to stare.

The sanctuary was divided into different sections. There were the kennels, a cattery, a Special Care unit, a horses and ponies section, and goats. Everybody had their favourite section to work in, and the manager did her best to keep us happy.

I wasn't confident in the kennels. Some of the dogs had been abandoned or abused, but others had been given to the charity because they were problem dogs. I now know that a 'problem dog' is rare; it's far more likely that the owner is at fault and is to blame for a dog's bad behaviour. However, the dogs seemed to sense my lack of confidence.

One of the long-term residents of the kennels was a Jack Russell named Pepper. He had a slightly deformed leg, probably as a result of abuse, and was renowned for his bad temper. He had bitten most members of staff. As soon as I approached his kennel, his lips would peel back and a low snarl rumbled from his depths. If I stepped closer, he would explode into a bristling, snapping demon, hurling himself at the wire fence in a frenzied attempt to shred me into little pieces.

"I don't know how you cope with Pepper," I said to Big Denise, another worker, one day. "I can't get near him, I'm sure he wants to kill me."

Denise was hugely overweight, but along with pies and cake, she adored animals.

"Pepper?" she asked. "He's a lovely boy, as long as you don't show any fear. Come and watch how nice he can be."

I hid as Denise approached his kennel. Pepper was lying down, chin on his paws, eyes watchful. The second he saw Denise, he leapt up, his lips already drawing back, daring her to come closer.

"Hello Pepper, how are you doing? Good boy! Fancy a walk?"

Pepper stood stock still, staring as she came closer. But he wasn't snarling.

"Good boy!" said Denise as she reached his door and unlocked it.

Pepper's ridiculous white stump of a tail began to twitch, then wagged furiously.

"Good boy!" said Denise as she snapped his leash to his collar. "Come on, boy, let's go for a walk."

And off they both trotted, Big Denise waddling and Pepper limping but happy.

I tried to copy Denise's example, but Pepper wasn't having any of it. As soon as I appeared, he became Demon Dog again. It wasn't just me, he was the same with every member of staff except Denise, and I'm afraid he didn't get walked on Big Denise's days off.

I helped to hose out and disinfect empty dogs' kennels, but I rarely worked with the dogs themselves. This suited me, as there were other sections in the sanctuary I much preferred to work in.

One section I particularly enjoyed was the Special Care unit. Apart from two long-term residents, one never knew what creatures were going to be in need of special care. Many of our patients were native Dorset wildlife.

All too often we had orphaned baby hedgehogs found by members of the public after their mother had been struck by a car. These little things, or hoglets as they are called, were helpless and would have died without our care. Most were so tiny that a whole litter of four or five could easily fit in one hand. They were adorable with their little pink hands and feet and their soft beige spines.

Each baby needed to be fed a special milk formula, and there was no room for mistakes. The formula had to be dissolved, but never whisked, or it would add too much air to their tiny tummies.

I was taught to warm the feed to room temperature and then deliver it by placing the baby on a towel on my lap. It was tempting to put the hoglet on its back, but we were taught to keep them the right way up, on their feet, to prevent them from inhaling the feed and drowning.

Then, very gently, we pressed the plunger of the syringe so the feed squeezed out drop by drop. Some hoglets took ages to get the idea and meals were a long process. Others attacked the syringe with gusto, guzzling the feed as though desperate. We had to keep it slow and steady, even with the greedy, excited ones.

After a meal, the tiniest hoglets needed to be toiletted, and as they had no mother to help, it was our job. We dipped a cotton bud in almond oil and gently stimulated the area under the tail to encourage them.

A hoglet

Baby hedgehogs are very cute and I discovered their favourite place to be was up my sleeves. If I put my hands in their box, they'd make a beeline for my sleeves. If I let them, and there was enough space, they would snuggle down in there and fall asleep. Extracting them, however, was much more challenging. They refused to leave and suddenly became all spiky and difficult to handle.

Of course the baby hedgehogs grew fast and it wasn't long before they no longer fitted up my sleeve. However, if I kept my arm still for long enough, the hedgehogs would content themselves by thrusting just their heads up my sleeve, leaving the rest of themselves hanging out. Then they'd sigh, settle down and fall asleep.

Hedgehogs may be wild creatures, but our baby hedgehogs still had to be introduced slowly to their natural surroundings. Having been raised and weaned indoors, they hadn't yet encountered grass and soil. It was our job to introduce them.

I would gently place them on the grass and watch. Bug-eyed with surprise, at first the babies stood stock still. Then they tried walking but the grass made it difficult and they clearly didn't like it. I could almost hear them thinking, *How do I get off this horrible stuff?* Then they'd pelt towards my feet and clamber up, gripping my laces with their tiny claws.

Once established on their shoe island in the middle of the sea of grass, they became a little braver. First one, then another would sniff the blades of grass, and even taste them. Then they would test it again with their feet, always making sure at least one foot was on my shoe in case of emergencies. This continued for a while but after a few visits, the babies became more confident and romped outside as happily as in.

Many baby birds were brought to our sanctuary by rescuers and we had a success rate of about 50%. Some had fallen out of their nests and needed constant feeding. Others were rescued from the jaws of a cat or dog and brought to us. It was always sad when we lost a little bird, but a triumph when we succeeded, when the baby thrived and was eventually set free.

Unfortunately, many well-meaning rescuers don't know that a baby bird with all his feathers is usually a fledgeling, and isn't necessarily needing help. He hasn't fallen out of the nest at all. He's ready to take the big step into the outside world. It's a dangerous time but he needs a couple of days on the ground. If the would-be rescuer leaves the little thing alone and watches, he'll probably see the fledgeling's mother appearing to feed him and teach him how to survive.

Sometimes we cared for deer that had been knocked down by cars. They were difficult patients because they often died of shock, even when their injuries weren't extensive.

The Special Care unit was where pregnant rescue cats and dogs came to give birth to their litters. One of our jobs was to fuss and play with the pups and kittens, to socialise them, and make them familiar with human handling. Being paid to play with puppies and kittens? I couldn't believe my luck!

In addition, there were two long-term residents of the Special Care unit. Sandy and Gordon had already been at the sanctuary for years before I joined, and stayed after I left.

20
Gordon the Gannet

Sandy was a large, affectionate golden retriever and was beloved by us all. In turn, he loved everybody and was happiest leaning against somebody's leg as they stroked his head and played with his soft ears. Only Pepper, the vicious Jack Russell with the deformed leg, had been in the sanctuary longer.

Anyone meeting or looking at him would never guess there was anything wrong with him, but poor Sandy was an epileptic. Several times a day, he would freeze, and his soft brown eyes would glaze over, the signal that another fit was imminent. Then his body would go stiff and he'd fall to the ground on his side. Now he had lost control. He foamed at the mouth and his body jerked as he paddled with all four limbs. It was heartbreaking to see, and there was nothing we could do to help him. The fits generally lasted between 30 and 90 seconds but seemed to go on for ever. When the seizure subsided, Sandy was left confused and disoriented, and in need of much petting and reassurance.

The fits were so frequent, it was considered most unlikely that Sandy would ever find a new home. So he was kept in the Special Care unit where we could keep an eye on and give him as much attention as he needed.

The other permanent patient was very different. Gordon, the gannet, (otherwise known as Thatbloodygreatbadtemperedseabird) was a big character at the sanctuary. Apart from an emu I met briefly many years later, Gordon was probably the most foul-tempered bird I have ever encountered. He had been found on a beach, exhausted, being tormented by a couple of dogs. A lady happened to be walking along the waterline and saw what was going on.

"Hey! Clear off!" she shouted at the dogs. "Leave that bird alone!"

The dogs ran off and she looked down at the bird. He didn't look injured, but he couldn't fly and she was determined not to desert him.

"Okay, bird," she said, approaching Gordon. "I'm going to pick you up, put you in my car and take you to the vet for a check over."

Gordon glared at her.

Before she could even reach down, Gordon's razor-sharp beak slashed her hand.

"Okay, bird," she said, mopping her bleeding hand with a handkerchief, "let's do this another way."

Gordon glared at her.

137

The lady unzipped her jacket and threw it over Gordon. Gordon squawked, but she managed to wrap him up and secure his wicked beak. She carried him to her car and took him straight to the local vet.

Luckily, there was no queue, and she and Gordon were admitted right away.

"Ah, so you've brought me some sort of seabird, have you?" asked the vet, staring at the webbed feet protruding from the jacket. "Just pop him on the table."

"He's got a very…"

Too late. As the vet tugged off the jacket, Gordon's beak was free. He whipped it round and took a chunk out of the vet's hand.

"…sharp beak," finished the lady.

The vet called his nurse.

"Brenda, could you restrain this lady's gannet please, while I attend to my cut hand and the gannet owner's cut hand?"

He disinfected and bandaged both their wounds, then addressed himself to Gordon. Gordon's beak was now taped shut but that didn't stop him glaring balefully at all three of them.

"Oh, he's a gannet is he?" asked the lady. "And he's not mine, I just found him on the beach being barked at and tormented by a couple of dogs."

"Did he try to fly?"

"No, not that I saw."

The vet unfurled Gordon's wings, one after the other and examined each closely.

Gordon's eyes narrowed in threat.

"Well, I can't see anything wrong with his wings. Or the rest of him. I'd say he's a young bird and he got caught in that storm last night. I think he's exhausted. A good rest and feed and he'll be as right as rain."

"I can't look after him," said the lady. "I know nothing about gannets and I have to go to work. Can I leave him here?"

Gordon's eyes became evil slits.

"I'm afraid we can't take him either," said the vet. "I suggest you drop him off at the animal sanctuary. Tell them he needs a rest and a feed, and I'm sure they'll look after him then set him free in a few days when he's got his strength back again."

The lady very kindly did exactly that. She delivered Gordon to the animal sanctuary, and relayed what the vet had said.

"Be careful," she warned. "His beak is lightning fast. He's already drawn blood twice!" She pointed to her bandaged hand. "He got me and he got the vet, too."

Gordon blinked malevolently.

"Well, I must be off. I'll leave you to it," she said, and left.

The Special Care unit manager, Simon, found a vacant pen with an empty pond which he reckoned would do nicely for Gordon's short stay.

"This'll do, Tony," he said to his long-haired assistant. "I'll pop out and buy some fish for him, and we'll fill his pond up tomorrow. He should be good to release in a few days."

Never work with children or animals; they'll always surprise you.

A gannet in the wild

Tony the Hippy was very careful and managed to release Gordon's beak without mishap. He left Gordon glaring round his temporary pen and waited for Simon to return. Simon arrived back from the fishmonger with a selection of fish for Gordon.

"How's Gordon been?" he asked.

"Cool, man, groovy."

Tony quickly chopped up the fish.

"I'll try him with this," said Simon and entered the pen.

He dumped the fish onto the ground, watching Gordon's reaction. Gordon peered at the mound of fish.

"I think he's interested," Simon said to Tony.

But Gordon wasn't interested. Next morning the mound of fish was exactly as they'd left it, except it was crawling with flies and beginning to smell.

The worldwide web hadn't yet been invented. In those days, if one wanted to research a subject, one had to go to the library, or buy a book about it, or ask an expert.

There wasn't a library close to hand, or a bookshop. They didn't know any gannet experts, so they did the next best thing, they phoned the vet.

"Could you tell us what gannets eat, please?"

"Hmm… Seawater fish, of course. I'm guessing mackerel and local species. Hasn't he eaten anything?"

"Nothing."

"Oh," said the vet suddenly. "I've just remembered something from my student days. I believe you need to keep the fish whole, don't cut them up. Did you chop them up?"

"Yes, we did."

"Right, keep them whole in future, heads, tails, everything. Then grab the tail and waggle it like mad so that the bird thinks its alive. They're not attracted to dead fish."

"Oh! Right! We'll try that then."

"Take care, his beak is really sharp."

"Don't worry, he hasn't tried anything with us yet."

Simon was hopeful and shot out to buy some fresh, whole, local, fish. He returned with a bag full, their tails poking out of the top.

"Let's see if this'll tempt him," said Simon. "Do you want to try, or shall I?"

"Hey, man, I'll have a go," said Tony the Hippy.

He grabbed a fish, let himself into Gordon's pen and crouched down. Holding the fish firmly by the tail, he waggled it in Gordon's direction. Gordon eyed him warily from the other side of the pen.

"He's watching," said Simon, "keep waggling!"

Gordon shrugged his shoulders, then started lumbering towards Tony and the fish, his webbed feet slapping the ground.

"Yes!" said Simon. "He's interested! He's coming over! Keep waggling the fish!"

Gordon was gathering momentum and moving faster now, heading for Tony and the fish, a gleam in his eye.

"Come on, man," said Tony encouragingly. "You must be starving, come and take a big bite."

Gordon reached the fish, stretched out his neck … and took a chunk out of Tony's hand.

"Ow!" yelled Tony, jumping back with more energy than hippies usually display. "Listen, you bloody over-sized seagull, I was just trying to feed you!"

Tony needed first aid for the nasty cut that Gordon had inflicted.

"Hey," he told me much later, holding out his hand for me to see. "I still have the scar."

And Gordon still hadn't been fed. Simon phoned the vet again and told him the latest developments.

"Looks like you'll have to force feed him," said the vet. "You'll need to push the fish down his neck. About three or four good-sized fish. Every day."

This wasn't good news for the staff or Gordon, but it needed to be done. Simon and Tony worked out the best way to do it, and it was a two-man job requiring sturdy gloves.

This was the procedure:

- Using a board, herd Gordon into a corner of his pen.
- Grab Gordon's neck with one hand, and his beak in the other.
- Kneel astride Gordon, to keep him still and his powerful wings folded, whilst still holding onto his beak. (Gannets have a wingspan of up to two metres, or six and a half feet.)
- Pull his beak open, pointing up, so that the fish will go straight down the neck.
- Ram the fish down Gordon's throat.

Poor Gordon. It was a terribly undignified operation and can't have been comfortable. However, it worked, and Gordon grew stronger, although his temper never improved.

Simon and Tony hoped that, when his pond was filled with water, Gordon might become more contented. They ran a hose into the pen and began to fill the pond. Gordon backed away to the far corner, glaring at the hose as though it was a vicious serpent. Even when the pond was filled to the brim and the hosepipe removed, he refused to come out of his corner.

"Hey man, what's the matter with that dude now?" asked Tony. "I thought he'd go and have a paddle at least."

But Gordon hated his pond and wouldn't go near it.

The next surprise came the following day. Having been force-fed several fish, Gordon was squirting all over the place, and his pen was a mess. Tony decided to hose everything down and pulled on his wellington boots and thick gloves in preparation. He let himself into the pen.

Gordon glared at him and the hosepipe.

Tony switched on the water and aimed a jet at the ground, washing Gordon's messes away.

Gordon, shivering, shrank into the corner as far away as possible. Tony needed to finish the job and did so as quickly as he could, not wanting to distress the bird.

"Hey, you know what?" he remarked to Simon later. "I reckon that gannet is afraid of water."

"That's ridiculous."

Ridiculous it may have been, but Gordon the Gannet turned out to be an anorexic, aquaphobic, human-hating, non-flying seabird. How had he, a bird who wouldn't fly and hated water, survived in the wild at all? It was a puzzling question.

Gordon couldn't be released; he had come to stay. They drained the water out of his pond and he was much happier, although he had to endure the daily hosing out of his pen. He never fed himself and had to be force-fed daily.

Gannets live between 17 and 37 years so Gordon became the longest staying permanent resident in the sanctuary, even longer than Sandy the epileptic golden retriever or Pepper, the limping, confrontational Jack Russell. When I arrived at the sanctuary, Gordon had already been there some time, and he was still going strong, slashing anyone who came too close, after I left. I was never allowed near him as I was a casual worker and not insured against his onslaughts.

How did I know Gordon's story in such detail? I knew because I had found my first 'proper' boyfriend, a fellow member of staff at the sanctuary.

Dorset Mackerel with Gooseberries

Gooseberries grow well in Dorset and mackerel are locally caught. Served together, they make a delicious dish, the gooseberries offering a wonderful zingy contrast to the rich fish.

Serves 4

15g (½ oz) butter
225g (8 oz) gooseberries, topped and tailed
4 mackerel, each weighing about 350g (12 oz), cleaned and with the heads removed
Salt and pepper
Lemon juice, to taste
1 egg, beaten

- First cook the gooseberries by melting the butter in a saucepan and adding the fruit. Cover tightly and cook over a low heat. Shake the pan occasionally, until the gooseberries are tender.
- Meanwhile, season the mackerel inside and out with salt, plenty of pepper and lemon juice.
- Make two or three slashes in the skin on each side of the fish, then grill for 15 - 20 minutes, depending on size, turning once, until tender.
- Puree the gooseberries in a blender or food processor. Use a fine sieve to ensure you have removed all the gooseberry pips.
- Pour the puree into a clean pan, beat in the egg, then reheat gently, stirring.
- Season to taste.
- Place the mackerel on warmed serving plates and spoon the sauce around the fish.

21
Tony the Hippy

Although Bournemouth was, and still is, a favourite destination for the retired, it is also a centre for language students. My school friends lived in the Poole district, and I lived even further away, in Wareham, but Bournemouth was where the action was, and where we could go to discos and meet boys.

We had a number of favourite haunts where we'd go on Friday and Saturday nights. Top of the list was probably Le Kilt, where admission was often free for girls. We spent all week at school planning and discussing what we were going to wear, then arrived dressed up to the nines. There, as the music blasted out James Brown and the Bee Gees, we met and danced with an assortment of students from all over the world.

As Le Kilt was in Bournemouth, it was difficult for me because I lived so far away. Luckily, Jo often invited me back to her house and we would get ready together. Sometimes I stayed the night, or I caught the milk train back to Wareham in the early hours of the morning. It cost me nothing as I had a season ticket because I caught the train to school every day.

We met a huge variety of foreign boys. I remember one Libyan boy, who I dated once, giving me a present. I was really pleased with it and took it home.

"*Ach,* what is that terrible smell?" asked my mother soon after.

I sniffed the air.

"What does it smell like?" I asked.

"It smells like a very big old dog has sneaked into the house and died," she said.

I raised my eyebrows in surprise.

"Yes, like a very *smelly* dog," she said, wrinkling her nose. "You haven't brought home a stray dog?"

"Of course not!"

"Humph! Something is making that smell."

She prowled around the house, sniffing the air until her nose led her up the staircase.

"It's getting stronger!"

She quickened her pace then sniffed her way into my bedroom.

"I found it!" she crowed in triumph, then pointed. "What is that on your bed, may I ask?"

All heaped up, it *did* look a bit like a big scruffy dog, or some other large animal. But it wasn't. It was my new Afghan coat.

For those who are unfamiliar with the Afghan coat, I will explain. It is a sheepskin or goatskin coat made with the fleece on the inside and the soft suede-like leather on the outside. It is often exquisitely embroidered with highly coloured silk thread. Afghan coats were first sold on London's Kings Road in 1966, where they were discovered, worn and made famous by the Beatles.

Good Afghan coats are cured and tanned professionally. However, numerous bad imitations flooded the market. These were coarsely embroidered and poorly cured. The Afghan coat I was given was definitely one of the latter. Most of the time it was inoffensive and smelt of nothing, but woe betide if I wore it in the rain. Then it became a reeking, fetid monster. It smelled so bad that my mother made me hang it in the garden shed; it wasn't allowed in the house.

I wonder whatever happened to that Afghan coat? It became so lively after getting damp that it may well have walked itself back to Afghanistan.

I had other colourful boyfriends who also gave me strange exotic gifts, but I lost my heart properly for the first time to Tony the Hippy, one of the permanent workers at the animal sanctuary.

With hindsight, it was all very one-sided. I would watch Tony as he mixed Sandy's dog food, and my heart would lurch. But Tony never noticed me.

"Hey, give this to Sandy," he would say, passing me the bowl.

If our fingers touched, it felt like an electric spark had arced between our hands. I froze, savouring the moment.

"For Sandy," he repeated, looking at me as though I didn't have both metaphorical oars in the water.

"Yes. For Sandy," I repeated.

I gulped and turned away, my face on fire.

Tony the Hippy wore his dirty blonde hair long and he sported a bristly moustache like Peter Starstedt. Beads swung around his neck and his jeans were flared and tattered. His floral shirts bore slogans of peace. I thought he was wonderful. I would find any excuse to work in the Special Care unit so I could be near him, but he never noticed me.

Being a permanent member of staff, Tony lived on-site in an old caravan. It was propped up on a pile of bricks, knee-deep in weeds. When Tony was off-duty, I would hear the strains of Bob Dylan or Joan Baez floating from his window, along with wafts of strange-smelling cigarette smoke. Sometimes he'd strum along to the music on his own guitar, and I would listen mesmerised. But he never noticed me.

Then one day, a strange thing happened. It was Tony's day off and he was sitting on the doorstep of his caravan. I passed, carrying a bag of fish destined for Gordon, the gannet. I gave Tony a small smile, all I could manage being so shy.

"Hey, Vicky," he said, "is that fish you've got there? For Gordon?"

I nodded.

"What's he got today? Mackerel?"

"I'm not sure," I said, and tried to open the bag to peer in.

"Gordon likes mackerel," said Tony, making conversation. "Well, as much as he likes any fish…"

Somehow, I was all fingers and thumbs and before I knew it, the plastic bag had slipped from my grasp and the fish spilled out and tumbled to the ground.

"Oh!"

Tony sprang forward and helped me capture the slithery, scaly things and push them back into the bag.

We both stood up at the same moment.

"There you go, that's the last one," he said, looking straight into my eyes.

For the first time, I gazed straight back, unblinking.

"Has anybody ever told you that you have the most beautiful, unusual green-coloured eyes?" he said, as though he'd just made a new discovery.

No, nobody has ever told me that, but I'm not going to admit it.

"Thank you."

"Hey, I was wondering… What are you doing after work tonight?"

I pretended to consider, but my heart was racing so fast I was sure he could hear it.

"Um, nothing. I, um, I believe I'm free tonight."

And that's how it all began. Romance blossomed over a carrier bag full of mackerel. It wasn't exactly how I imagined it would happen; there were no sunsets, or butterflies, or birdsong, just some smelly dead fish and a slimy carrier bag.

Tony and I quickly became inseparable. I began to part my hair in the middle and even wore headbands and dangly earrings. I embraced vegetarianism and wore faded flared jeans and smocks. I would have taken up smoking weed in clay pipes but it made me cough. On my days off and during my lunch breaks, I lounged on the orange and purple geometric cushions in Tony's caravan, listening to Bob Dylan and Joan Baez.

Working at the animal sanctuary was always fun, but now I just couldn't wait to get to work every day. The first pleasure of the day was opening my locker. Tony often scribbled little notes, folded them in half and slotted them through the crack in my locker door. Sometimes the note just had a silly joke, like:

How do you know you're in bed with an
elephant?
Because of the 'E' embroidered on his
pyjamas.
Hehehe!
Love,
T xxx

But other notes made my knees go weak, and I would stuff those into my bra, next to my heart, to re-read a thousand times that day.

Vicky, I couldn't get to sleep last night
thinking about your green eyes. Can't wait to
see you today,
All my love,
T xxx

Luckily, it was the school holidays, so I was there most of the time. Tony and I held hands or embraced in secret, and for a while, the sky became bluer, and the grass greener. I was seventeen and in love, with the world at my feet.

Tony's family lived in Birmingham, and I loved to listen to the 'Brummy' twang in his voice. I teased him when he used words and phrases unfamiliar to us southerners.

"Our kid is doing really well at school," he said.

"Our kid? You have a child?"

"No! Our kid is me younger brother."

Then he'd tease me back when I used Dorset slang words like 'grockles' meaning tourists.

Tony was several years older than I was, and although he had qualifications, he didn't know what he wanted to do with his life. I was studying for my 'A' levels and planned to go to Teacher Training College. I imagined Tony would stay in Dorset, waiting for me to finish. Then I would come back and we would live happily ever after.

Then one day, Tony dropped a bombshell that rocked my teenage world.

"I've applied for university and been accepted."

In those days, 'Gap Years' hadn't been given the name yet. Usually, when one left school, one immediately went to university, college, or on to a chosen career. It was very unusual for anybody to spend a year or more 'experiencing' the world before they entered university or the serious world of work. Tony had decided he needed some time out of education, which was why he was working at the animal sanctuary, although I didn't know that then. I guess I thought that the animal sanctuary would be his career.

"University?"

"Yes. In Birmingham where my family come from. I've handed in my notice here. I'm leaving tomorrow and going on holiday with my family first."

"What?"

Shock robbed me of words.

"This is my last week. I'm sorry. I knew you'd be upset so I've been keeping it from you."

"Birmingham? *Birmingham?* But what about us?"

Silence.

That silence told me all I needed to know. There was no 'us'. I didn't figure in Tony's future.

"How long have you known?"

"A long time. I just couldn't face telling you."

His hands were gripping my arms but I threw him off.

"You've known all this time? How *could* you!"

I turned on my heel and left him standing there, smoothing his bristly moustache down with his forefinger. I burst into Sandy's pen, flung my arms round the old retriever's neck, and buried my face in his golden fur.

The next day I phoned in sick. There was no way I could face Tony, no way I could say goodbye to him. I felt as though somebody had stamped on my heart.

I scraped my hair back and stared at myself in the mirror. *I will never trust a man again,* I told myself. *I will never eat again. I may shave my head. I'll just languish here in my bedroom, nursing my broken heart. He'll be sorry when he hears I've died of a broken heart. And if they force-feed me like they do Gordon the Gannet, and I survive, I'll never go into the outside world again. I'll stay here like Miss Haversham, gathering dust.*

"*Ach,* how are you feeling?" asked my mother, popping her head round the door. "Mrs James at Cullens says there's a nasty bug going round, you've probably caught that."

"I think I'm going to die," I announced with a quaver in my voice.

"*Ach,* I don't think it's that bad, just a tickly cough and a bit of a sore throat. I'll make you some semolina to soothe your throat."

"No food," I said feebly. "I can't face any food."

How can semolina mend a broken heart?

"Okay," she said and left me alone.

I heard her go down the stairs and close the back door. I knew she was on her way to check her compost heap.

"Nobody understands," I whispered, burying my face in my pillows.

All those daydreams where he and I would walk off together into the sunset to save the world...

All that paper I had wasted at school doodling his name and practising writing my signature, *Mrs Victoria Fletcher*....

All for nothing. He didn't care about me.

If I survive, I'm going to become a nun.

By the next day, I was starving, and rather bored with being in my own bedroom for so long. *Okay, I'll eat,* I relented, *but my vegetarian days are over.*

"Glad you are feeling better," said my mother. "I didn't think you'd be eating anything much yet, so I haven't prepared any vegetables for you. We've got sausage pie."

"That's okay."

"But you are vegetarian?"

"Not any more."

The sausage pie tasted great and I had a double helping on principle, just to spite Tony. But I didn't feel any better for my traitorous behaviour.

I stopped listening to Bob Dylan and played Simon and Garfunkel records instead. Tears of self-pity coursed down my cheeks as I played *Bridge over Troubled Water* again and again.

When I went back to work, two big things happened.

First, I found a note that had been pushed into my locker through the crack in the door. My heart lurched and I held my breath as I unfolded it. He'd changed his mind! He wanted me back!

> *Dear Vicky,*
> *I'm sorry it had to end this way. It's my fault,*
> *I should have told you I was planning to go*
> *to uni. I hope we can stay friends. I'm going*
> *to be popping into the sanctuary to say*
> *goodbye properly before I leave for the new*
> *term. I hope to see you then.*
> *Tony*

Huh! No kisses? No 'I miss you' or even 'All my love'? Friends? What was the point of that? I had already designed the wedding dress. I was going to borrow my mother's pearls and wear a blue garter. I planned on spending the rest of my life with Tony and he had snatched my dreams away. He didn't deserve my friendship, and I certainly wasn't going to look out for his visit.

But I was lying to myself. During public visiting times, when the gates opened, I would search the visitors, always hoping Tony the Hippy would be amongst the sea of faces.

The second big thing that happened was that the schedule had been changed. According to the new schedule pinned to the noticeboard, no longer would I be working in the Special Care unit. Instead, I would be working in the cattery.

Quick & Easy Sausage and Mash Pie

Serves 2

5 sausages
1 onion (cut in half if large)
Gravy granules
Tomato puree
3 potatoes (good size)
Handful of mushrooms
Red wine
Powdered garlic, salt and pepper
Grated cheese, (optional)

Method

- Chop the onion, sausages, and mushrooms and place in a pan with some oil.
- Put potatoes on to boil and take them off when tender (approx 15 mins).
- When the sausages are cooked, add a dash of gravy granules and tomato puree and stir together with the sausages, onions and mushrooms.
- Add pepper, salt, some garlic powder and red wine for taste.
- Cook it all until the potatoes are ready to be mashed. Mash them, and put the sausage mixture into a casserole dish.
- Put mashed potato on top, sprinkle with grated cheese and pop under the grill until the cheese turns golden brown and bubbles.

22
Cats

Being told that I'd been moved out of the Special Care unit would normally have plunged me into a deep depression as I would have been separated from my beloved Tony. He had abandoned me without a backward glance to explore distant exotic shores (well, Birmingham), so I was pleased not to have to work where there were constant reminders of him. No longer would I have to walk past Tony's old caravan, which was now occupied by Big Denise.

Yes, working in the cattery would suit me fine.

I love cats. I love their individuality and their general snootiness. I've had cats as pets since, but I've always felt that they owned me, not vice versa. I hadn't realised how many different shapes, colours, sizes and personalities of domestic cat existed in the world until I worked in the cattery at the animal sanctuary.

The cattery was made up of a long line of pens. Each outdoor part had structures to climb, or hide in, and a basket for its occupant to snooze in the sun. A little doorway led to an indoor compartment with more snug beds and different levels to climb. It was pussycat paradise, but not freedom.

Kittens were usually re-homed very quickly. The more mature feline residents had to wait until they were noticed, although the sanctuary did its best to make their lives pleasant.

Each cat had a story, and many were found as strays, like Hamworthy.

"Why is he called Hamworthy?" I asked Big Denise who was showing me the ropes.

"He was found trying to stow away in the First Class compartment of a train on the London Waterloo line. The stationmaster discovered him at Hamworthy junction."

Hamworthy rubbed his ginger cheek on my leg and purred. I scratched him behind the ear and his eyes glazed in pleasure.

"And Seafore? I guess he was found on the beach or something?"

"Nope. It should be 'C for' really. C for cat. We'd run out of name ideas when he came in."

"Oh. And Carpenter?"

"Ah, poor old Carpy isn't very bright. He has never really been properly house-trained. I expect somebody dumped him because of that. We call him Carpenter because he's always doing little jobs around the place."

"Jobs?"

"Yes, smelly ones."

"Oh."

Work in the cattery was very simple. I had to go from pen to pen, cleaning them out and replacing the cat litter. I made sure the drinking water was fresh and clean, and filled the food bowls morning and evening. Any spare time I had, I could spend stroking and playing with the inmates.

Some of the cats were so shy that they'd vanish into their indoor sleeping quarters as soon as I appeared. Others didn't flee, but watched me with one wary eye cracked open. If I attempted to stroke them, they were gone.

Some of the cat pens were empty with the doors propped open. The cats living in these pens were there on a Dinner, Bed and Breakfast basis. They were very tame and allowed to roam freely around the sanctuary during the day, returning to be fed and shut in at night.

A few cats in the closed pens were friendly, almost tripping me up as they wound themselves around my ankles as I tried to carry out my chores. The cat I remember most clearly, and with huge guilt, was a little tabby cat called Blossom.

Blossom lived in a closed pen with three much shyer kitties. As soon as I arrived, she twisted figures of eight around my ankles, clamouring for attention. I rubbed under her chin, which she loved, and behind her ears. If I had time, I would sit with her awhile and she'd climb into my lap, purring like an industrial lawnmower.

"Why don't we allow Blossom out of her pen during the day?" I asked Big Denise, who had recently been promoted to Assistant Manager. "She's so friendly and affectionate. I'm sure she'd love the extra interaction with the staff and visitors. She might even find someone to adopt her."

"I'm not sure," said Denise. "There must be a reason for her being kept in a closed pen."

Over the next few days I brought up the subject whenever I could.

"I think it's unfair," I declared. "Poor Blossom."

"If you are sure she's so tame," said Denise, a little doubtfully, "perhaps we could let her out on trial and see what happens."

"Fantastic! Now?"

"Yes, why not?"

Together we walked to Blossom's pen. As usual, her three shy roommates streaked away into their indoor quarters, while Blossom came forward to greet her admirers.

"You're a lovely little cat, aren't you?" crooned Denise, stroking Blossom until she purred like a pneumatic drill. "Would you like a taste of freedom?"

"You see how tame she is?" I said.

"Yup. She knows you, why don't you pick her up and take her outside, see how she likes it?"

I picked Blossom up and cuddled her. She purred even louder. I walked out through the door, closing it behind me with my foot to prevent her roommates from escaping.

The purring stopped abruptly. I felt Blossom stiffen. Then she exploded out of my arms and hit the ground running. Denise and I watched in horror as she streaked across the field and disappeared into a hedge.

"Oh no," we said, staring in disbelief, first at each other, then at the distant hedge.

"Blossom! Blossom! Here, kitty, kitty!"

But no amount of searching, calling, or coaxing flushed Blossom out of her hiding place.

We mentioned the incident in the staffroom.

"Blossom?" asked one of the old-timers, mid-sandwich. "Little tabby cat, very friendly?"

We nodded.

"Oh, she's agoraphobic. Doubt you'll ever see her again."

Denise and I were horrified, but although we never gave up searching, nobody ever saw Blossom again.

Racked with guilt, I vowed that in future I would never again interfere. Never would I assume that I knew better. However, I'm afraid, looking back on my life, I acknowledge that I've often meddled in affairs that were none of my business. I should have learned my lesson from what befell little Blossom.

In spite of the loss of little Blossom, I had found my niche working in the cattery. I loved them all, but of course I had my favourites.

I loved Marmite, the sneaky, handsome, coal-black cat who liked to jump out at me from behind corners, then wind himself around my ankles in apology. I loved Frosty, the deaf white cat with no ears, a skin cancer victim who still lived life to the full in spite of her misfortune. She loved to doze in sun puddles and rolled luxuriously onto her back to have her tummy rubbed whenever I approached. But most of all, I loved Nig-Nog.

Poor Nig-Nog would never win a prize at a cat show because he was not a handsome cat. He was a huge boy, probably from a mixed heritage because his colouring ranged from splotches of white on his face, to hectic ginger stripes up two legs and brown patches over his back. It was as though his designer couldn't decide what colour he should be, and experimented with all of them. Even Nig-Nog's eyes were eccentric as he had one green and one yellow. But what Nig-Nog lacked in beauty, he made up for in personality, and he was one of the most endearing, comical cats I have ever met.

Nig-Nog didn't live in the cattery. He was his own boss, and chose to roam the sanctuary by day and sleep in the stables with the goats at night. I don't know how he knew the difference between weekdays and weekends, but every Saturday and Sunday morning he'd be waiting for the staff minibus to arrive. As soon as the driver applied the handbrake, Nig-Nog shot forward and circled the bus, looking for me. He would stand on his hind legs with his front paws on the side of the vehicle, his head tilted back as he stared through the windows searching for me.

When I jumped off the bus and called him, he would gallop forward to greet me, his head butting me in welcome. My fellow staff members rolled their eyes in amusement. Nig-Nog didn't like to be picked up, so I leaned down to stroke his head and talk to him. And that was another of Nig-Nog's endearing traits: he talked.

"Hello, Nig-Nog, how are you this morning?" I asked.

"Meowwww-purrp."

"Oh good. I hope you've been keeping those goats in order."

"Meoooow-meowwww."

"Right, and have you been sorting out the mice?"

"Purrrp-mew-meooow…"

And so on. Nig-Nog and I chatted all day, and wherever I was, he was only a scamper behind.

As I worked my way along the cattery pens, Nig-Nog would wait for me, not at the gates of the pens, but on the chicken-wire roof. His weight caused the roof to sag and it can't have been comfortable for him, but that was his chosen position, the place where he could keep a green or yellow eye on me.

Nig-Nog didn't know he was a cat. I'm not sure what he thought he was, but if I threw a little stick, he would dash to chase it and fetch it back. So perhaps he thought he was a dog.

At lunch times, I would often choose not to sit in the staffroom with the other workers. Instead, I would stretch out in the long grass at the edge of the pasture, staring up at the Dorset sky, sharing my sandwiches with Nig-Nog and telling him all my troubles.

"Can you believe that Tony could be such a rat, Nig-Nog?"

"Meooowww-purrp-meow."

"If he was really a rat you'd catch him for me, wouldn't you?"

"Purrrp-meoeeew."

"Thank you, I knew you would."

"Purrrp."

❁ ❁ ❁

154

During the school holidays I worked full-time at the animal sanctuary, and during term time, I just worked weekends. I should have been studying, but I set aside very little time for that. So when the offer of an additional part-time job came along, I seriously considered it.

"They were talking in Cullens," said my mother. "There's a waitress job going on the quay. It might suit you better than the animal sanctuary, it's much closer."

"I don't want to give up my job there," I said, "but perhaps I could do both?"

"*Ach,* what about your studying? You want to get into that Teacher Training college, you know."

I did know, but I didn't really care. At least when I was working, I didn't have time to think about Tony and the way his long hair curled over his shoulders, or brood over how horrible men were.

Wareham is an ancient, historic town situated on the River Frome which leads out to Poole Harbour. (The smaller River Piddle, whose name still makes me giggle, also flows past Wareham.) Excavations have produced axe heads and flint workings, evidence of settlements dated around 9000 BC. Up until the 12th or 13th century, Wareham had been quite a major port, but as the river began to silt up, most of the foreign trade transferred to Poole.

Although, as a youngster, I may not have appreciated it, I was aware that Wareham quay was extremely picturesque. Steeped in ancient Saxon and Roman history as it is, Wareham is a place that tourists flock to, and the quay is seldom quiet. A white arched bridge spans the Frome and the scene, with its little boats, historic buildings and water reflections has been reproduced on postcards countless times. My book-jacket designer, Nick Saltmer, chose to paint Wareham quay as the cover to this book.

There were, and still are, two pubs on the quay, The Quay Inn and The Old Granary. The job vacancy was for a waitress at The Old Granary, a lovely old building right beside the water. I already had a little experience waitressing, and therefore got the job, but I was never a good waitress.

The Old Granary offered a delicious menu which attracted a mixed clientele; some locals, some regulars and numerous tourists. Most of the customers were utterly polite and charming, particularly the Americans who gazed around wide-eyed, drinking in the history we Brits so take for granted.

However, I remember an instance with customers who were so rude, I never forgot them.

Crêpes Suzette

Serves 4 - 6

For the crêpes:
1 cup plain flour
2 eggs
½ cup milk
½ cup water
¼ teaspoon salt
2 tablespoons butter, melted

For the filling:
Juice of 2 oranges
Zest of 1 orange
175g (6 oz) butter
75g (2½ oz) caster sugar
80ml (3 fl oz) liqueur (for instance, Grand Marnier, Cointreau or Triple Sec)

Method

To make the crêpes:
- In a large mixing bowl, whisk together the flour and the eggs.
- Gradually add in the milk and water, stirring to combine.
- Add the salt and butter and beat until smooth.
- Heat a lightly oiled frying pan over medium high heat. Pour or scoop the batter in, using approximately ¼ cup of the mixture for each crepe. Tilt the pan with a circular motion so that the batter coats the surface evenly.
- Cook the crêpe for about 2 minutes, until the bottom is light brown.
- Loosen with a spatula, flip over and cook the other side.

The filling:
- Pour the orange juice into a saucepan, and add the zest, butter and sugar.
- Bring to the boil, and then turn the heat down to simmer for a further 15 minutes or until the sauce becomes sticky.
- Fold the crêpes and arrange them in a large pan so that they slightly overlap each other.
- Pour the warm syrup over the crêpes and then gently heat them for 3 minutes.
- Warm the liqueur in the emptied (but syrupy) saucepan.
- When the crêpes are hot, pour the liqueur over them and set light to the pan.

23
Gits and Goats

The Old Granary had a family atmosphere, so when I walked up to attend a particular table, I was surprised to see two men sitting there, staring at me belligerently.

"Good evening," I smiled. "I'm Vicky and I'll be serving you this evening."

"You don't look like a Vicky," said the one who was wearing a green shirt and a Mickey Mouse tie. "We'll call you Josephine."

"Josephine! Haw-haw, you look like a Josephine," said his companion, a balding man sporting one of those flashy new digital Casio watches.

I raised my eyebrows.

Well, they can call me whatever they like as long as they leave a decent tip, I thought.

I said nothing but my eyes strayed to a tower of 50 pence pieces in the middle of the white tablecloth.

"Ah," crowed Mickey Mouse, "you've noticed these little beauties then! That's your tip there, Josephine! There's five nice British pounds here, but every time you displease us, I'm going to take one away."

"Haw-haw!" guffawed Casio Watch.

My mouth dropped open.

"You're joking!" I blurted.

They weren't. Mickey Mouse's hand shot out and removed the top coin from the pile.

"Haw-haw!" guffawed Casio Watch. "Careful, Josephine! He did warn you!"

"You haven't given us a menu yet, Josephine," said Mickey Mouse, removing another 50 pence piece from the dwindling tower and slipping it back in his pocket.

Nothing went right.

The water jug was too full and splashed the cloth.

The wine was corked.

The food arrived too slowly.

There wasn't enough *vin* in the *coq au vin*.

The peas were overcooked.

"Oh *dear*, Josephine, you won't have much of a tip left unless you buck your ideas up," said Mickey Mouse, slipping yet another 50 pence piece into his pocket.

I'd already come to terms with the fact that I would not be earning a tip from this table. In my head, I called them the Gruesome Twosome, and it wasn't only their tipping strategy that irked me. Throughout their meal, they kept calling for me.

"Josephine! Over here! You haven't refilled the bread basket!"

"Josephine! Where's the tartare sauce?"

Then, when I served them, they wouldn't stop talking, even when I tried to back away to serve other tables. To make matters worse, Casio Watch invaded my personal space and grabbed my wrist, preventing me from getting away.

"Excuse me, I need to check your order in the kitchen," I protested, and tried to pull away.

By now, the Gruesome Twosome had consumed two bottles of wine between them and were even louder and more unruly.

"They are impossible!" I ranted to the other staff in the kitchen.

"They sound like a couple of gits," agreed the chef.

'Git' was a rude word, commonly used in Dorset, meaning a contemptible person. I thought it fitted the Gruesome Twosome perfectly.

"Josephine!" said Mickey Mouse, plucking at my apron ties as I served a neighbouring table.

"Are you going to give us a

Coq au Vin

Serves 4

8 cooked joints of chicken, on the bone - a mixture of breasts and thighs or legs
30g (1 oz) butter
1 tbsp olive oil
4 garlic cloves, chopped
2 red onions, sliced
250g (9 oz) button mushrooms
Good pinch of dried thyme
290ml (½ pint) red wine
500ml (17fl oz) fresh chicken stock
150m (1¼ pint) double cream
2 tbsp chopped fresh parsley
Salt and freshly ground black pepper

Method
- Skin the cooked chicken pieces and set aside.
- Heat the butter with the oil and add the garlic and onions.
- Sauté for about 5 minutes until softened.
- Add the mushrooms and thyme and sauté for a further 5 minutes.
- Pour in the wine, bring to the boil and continue boiling until the sauce is reduced by half.
- Pour in the stock and bring back to the boil.
- Season and add the chicken to the sauce.
- Simmer for 5 minutes until the chicken is thoroughly heated through.
- Remove the chicken pieces.
- Increase the heat and boil the sauce until reduced by half.
- Reduce the heat, stir in the cream and heat.
- Pour the sauce over the chicken pieces and sprinkle with parsley.

discount?"

"No," I said flatly, and saw the last 50 pence piece disappear into his pocket.

"Well! How very rude!" said Mickey Mouse, affronted. "And after we've been so nice to you, too! You mark my words, we'll *never* come back to this restaurant."

I cheered inwardly but said nothing as I watched them count out exactly the right money for the bill and leave it on the table. They were the last customers to leave. I stood with the other members of staff as they blundered their way out, bumping into tables, reaching the coat stand, collecting their jackets, stepping out onto the quay, and finally slamming the restaurant door behind them. Forgive me, but I hoped they'd fall into the River Frome. I wouldn't be jumping in to rescue them. Nasty little gits.

"Good riddance!" I muttered, then smiled to myself.

"Did they leave you a good tip?" asked the chef, catching my smile.

"No," I said, "but I left them one."

I wondered how long it would take them to find the fish heads I'd picked out of the kitchen dustbin and pushed into their coat pockets.

Would they work out where the fish heads had come from?

Of course they would.

Would they come back the next day and get me fired?

Probably.

I didn't care. It was worth it. And anyway, I had decided that waitressing was not for me. If I wanted to be a teacher, perhaps I should concentrate a little harder on my school work and passing my exams.

❈ ❈ ❈

I enjoyed my days in the cattery, but occasionally I would be asked to help in other departments, to cover for absent members of staff. Sometimes I took over the kennels but I was nervous of some of the dogs and I never attempted to take bad-tempered Pepper for a walk.

More often I'd help out at the goat stable, and the first time this happened, I needed to be taught what to do. Nobody was forced to work in any department, but I volunteered, thinking working with goats might be fun. Julie usually cared for the goats and she showed me what needed to be done.

The goats had their own large stable where they spent the night. The cement floor was lined with straw.

"Right," said Julie. "First thing in the morning, open the top half of the stable door and look inside. Check them out, make sure they all look okay. Take care, because goats are jumpers. If you're not careful, they'll take a flying leap at the door and try to escape."

"Okay," I said, as she demonstrated how to do it.

"Next," said Julie, "slip in, closing the door firmly behind you. Come on!"

I followed her closely. Julie swung the door closed and switched on the light. A dozen horned heads swung in our direction. A few of the braver ones stepped forward.

"Morning, goats!" said Julie. Then to me, "They are naturally curious, they'll come up and sniff you, and probably start chewing on your clothes, so watch out!"

Soon I was in the thick of the baaing, hard-headed herd. The goats stepped on my feet with their sharp hooves, and their long teeth plucked at my T-shirt.

"Quick!" said Julie. "Grab that little brown one by the horns before she skips away. That's Jemima. She has a phantom pregnancy and we need to milk her before we take the goats to their field."

I grabbed Jemima, and Julie pulled the little goat towards her, then leant her against the wall. Jemima's udders were tight, but a few expert squeezes from Julie relieved the pressure.

"You milk her every morning?" I asked.

"Yup! It's not hard though, as soon as you've caught her she'll let you do it."

"Okay, so what's next?"

"We need to get the whole herd out of the stable and down the lane to their field."

"Does anybody help?"

"Nope. There is only one way to do it and you only get one chance. When you open the stable door, they could run out and go left or right. We need to make sure they turn left, go down to the bottom of the lane, and turn into their field."

"How on earth do you do that with no help?"

"Goats are really inquisitive, and they love chasing things. Especially old Butch here." She scratched the head of a particularly large white-bearded goat beside her. "And if Butch runs, the whole herd will follow."

"So what does Butch chase after?"

"You."

I gaped at her.

"Me? Chase *me?*"

What? No dog to round them up or chase after?

"Yes, you. I do it every morning and evening. It's not difficult, you just need to know what to expect."

"So this is the only way to get the goats to their field?"

"Yup. You shouldn't have any problems. Big Denise can't do it, of course, because she can't run."

This conversation was not filling me with confidence and I suddenly wished I'd made more of an effort in PE at school.

"Right, first we need to get out of the stable without letting any goats out. Follow me."

We squeezed out and stood outside.

"Bring some carrots with you tomorrow, it'll make things much easier." She grabbed a bunch from a bucket by the door. "Now watch, and follow me closely. Do *everything* I do. When we get to the field, dart behind the gate."

Before I had time to ask any more questions, Julie swung open the upper half of the door.

"Goaties!" she called, jiggling the carrots. "Look what I've got!"

All the goats swung round and eyed the carrots.

"Come and get them!"

She threw open the lower section of the stable door, turned, and pelted down the lane. I sprinted after her, and right behind me galloped the herd of goats. It was only a short lane, with high hedges either side, but that day it felt a full mile long.

Once in the field, she flung the carrots as far as she could, then darted behind the gate, with me close on her heels. The goats galloped to the carrots, but Butch had reached them first and was already munching. The goats spun round, looking for Julie, the carrot provider.

"Quick, close the gate," panted Julie.

Together we pushed it closed, then leant on it, catching our breaths and watching the goats lose interest in us and begin to graze on the grass and hedges.

"And you do this every day?"

"Yup. Evenings are easier. You don't have to bribe them because they know there's a feed waiting for them in the stable. You still have to let them chase you though, otherwise they'd take all evening because they'd stop to graze the hedges, and some might wander off."

I sighed and wished that I'd never volunteered to help with the goats, and hoped tomorrow would never come.

Julie showed Nig-Nog and me how to muck out the stable and prepare the evening feed.

"You'll be fine tomorrow. Even if they catch you, they won't hurt you. They might head-butt you a bit, specially old Butch, but that's all."

"I'm really not looking forward to tomorrow," I told Nig-Nog later as I shared my cheese sandwich with him.

"Meooowww-purrrpp."

The next day arrived much too quickly. I made my way to the goat stable and let myself in, while Nig-Nog sat on the fence watching proceedings.

Catching Jemima proved easy, in spite of the other goats pushing and nuzzling me curiously, and old Butch searching my pockets. I was glad I'd left my carrots outside. Jemima let me grab her udder and I imitated Julie's action, pleased to see a few squirts of milk hit the straw at my feet.

Good. That was done. All I had to do now was slip out of the stable. Easy. My confidence was returning.

"All going well so far," I told Nig-Nog cheerily.

I grabbed the bunch of carrots from the bucket by the door, and took a deep breath before opening the upper section of the stable door.

"Goaties!" I called, holding the carrots up just like Julie had done. "Look what I've got!"

The goats all swung round and stared. Old Butch's eyes narrowed and he launched himself at the carrots. But I was too quick. Swiftly pulling back the bolt securing the bottom half of the door, I swung it open and tore down the lane as though my life depended on it, pursued by Butch and the entire goat herd.

Surely the lane was longer than yesterday? I could hear the hooves thundering behind me. I risked a glance over my shoulder, and that was my undoing. Somehow, I tripped over my own feet and stumbled. The ground came up to meet me.

Something snatched the carrots from my hand. Butch.

Sharp hooves pawed me. Whiskery faces nudged me.

I stood up quickly, furious with myself. Now what? Some of the goats had circled Butch, hoping for a bite of carrot, but the last traces were fast disappearing.

Quick! I had to act fast or the goats would start wandering. I patted my pockets, searching for inspiration. I had nothing except a red handkerchief. I drew it out.

"Goaties!" I yelled, waving the hanky. "Look what I've got!"

And then I ran.

The goats lifted their heads and stampeded after me. Seconds later I was in the field. The hanky was balled in my hand by now and I flung it as far as I could. It landed just a few feet away but still gave me enough time to get behind the gate and push it shut while the herd investigated the hanky.

"Whew! I did it!" I said aloud as I leaned on the gate looking back into the field.

Some goats had already lost interest, wandered off and busily cropped the long grass and dandelions. Butch was swallowing the last remnants of my red handkerchief. I sighed. That's why I loved this job; no two days were ever the same.

Working at the animal sanctuary, Nig-Nog, the cattery, and the goats, all filled my mind most of the time, but I still mourned the loss of Tony and just thinking about him would make my heart ache with hurt pride.

24
Surprising Visitors

In the afternoons, the sanctuary would open to visitors and we all hoped that some of our charges would find new homes.

It was unlikely that anybody would give homes to our retired pit ponies. These ponies were little more than 12 hands high and over twenty years old, unsuitable for riding.

Working conditions for pit ponies had improved over the years, but in the old days, shaft ponies were usually stabled underground, only surfacing during the colliery's annual holidays. They could work an eight-hour shift daily, during which they might haul 30 tons of coal. How wonderful it was to see them end their days cropping the lush Dorset grass. It's unbelievable and shameful to think that the last pit ponies were retired as late as the 1990s.

It was doubtful that anyone would re-home the retired beach donkeys, either. These plucky little beasts of burden had spent their lives trudging up and down the sands, giving children rides. At least the sanctuary could give them a peaceful retirement in the green fields of Dorset.

No, it was much more likely that visitors would adopt a cat or dog. The puppies and kittens in the Special Care unit never stayed long, somebody always fell in love with them and offered them a forever home. Sometimes the adult cats in my cattery found new homes, always a cause for celebration. Nobody ever wanted Nig-Nog, but I didn't mind that because he already enjoyed a good life, and was a favourite with the staff.

Occasionally one of the older dogs would find a home, which was always good news. However, there were some, like ferocious Pepper, who would never know what it was like to belong to someone. There was nothing endearing about the poor chap. Not only was he deformed, but his vicious snarl would chase any prospective owner away.

On one particular afternoon the visitors were milling round the animal sanctuary and families chatted as they viewed the cats and dogs in their pens. Big Denise was on hand to answer any questions when she noticed an elderly man leaning on his walking stick, staring at each dog in turn.

"Can I help you?" she asked. "Are you looking for a particular type of dog? We have small dogs over here, and…"

"No," said the old man, cutting her short. "I don't want any of these."

They had reached the end of the line. The old man turned to limp away, when he stopped suddenly.

"I can hear growling," he said, cupping his ear.

"Yes, I'm sorry, that's Pepper in the last pen. He hates visiting time. Actually, he hates everything and everyone. He's hiding in his kennel."

"I want to see him."

"Oh, Pepper wouldn't make a suitable pet at all, I'm sorry. He has a deformed leg and a terrible temper. I'm afraid he bites."

"I said I want to see him."

"I'm sorry, sir, but that just isn't possible."

The old man said no more but turned and stumped away.

Big Denise forgot all about him until she entered the kennel building a while later. Visitors viewing the animals could only do so from outside and were never allowed inside the building. A big sign - *Staff Only, No Unauthorised Entry* - was posted on the door. This door opened onto a long corridor from which each pen could be accessed, either on the left or the right.

To her astonishment, she could hear a man's low voice at the end of the corridor. Quietly, she approached.

"So you've got a bad leg, too, have you, old fella?" she heard the man say. "Well, bad-tempered old chaps like us should stick together."

And then Big Denise realised who the intruder was; the old man with the walking stick who she'd been talking to earlier.

"I'm sorry, sir, you're not allowed..." she started to say, but the words died before she could finish the sentence.

Not only had the old man entered the building, but he was sitting on a stool *inside* Pepper's enclosure. And what was Pepper doing? Pepper sat meekly in front of the old man, peering up into his face. One paw was on the old man's knee, and his eyes were half shut with pleasure as the old man fondled his ears.

"Just for a second," Big Denise told me, "I thought there was some mistake, that this wasn't our Pepper at all."

"So what happened next?" I asked, enchanted by the story.

"I watched them together for a while, and I had to admit, those two were made for each other. Pepper behaved like a different dog; gentle, patient and obedient. The old man told me he wanted to adopt Pepper, and I couldn't think of a single reason why he shouldn't."

"Right, old boy," said the old man as he let himself out of Pepper's pen. "I'm going to sign some papers and stuff, and then I'm going to arrange to take you home. You wait right there."

Pepper's stubby tail wagged so fast it was almost a blur.

So Pepper did find himself a new home after all. By the time the old man came to collect him the next weekend, the story had spread and all the staff came to wish the pair farewell. The old man removed Pepper's old collar with the animal sanctuary's tag on it, and placed a new blue collar round his neck, with a matching lead.

"There! Now you look very handsome!"

Pepper's stubby tail wagged in a frenzy and he licked the old man's hand.

"Right, old boy, that's it then. Say goodbye, let's take you home."

With a brief wave to us, the old man stumped away, leaning on his stick. Pepper trotted beside him, proud head up, limping slightly but with a noticeable new spring in his step.

We shook our heads and smiled, amazed. This wasn't the Pepper we knew and feared.

"Bye, and good luck," we called as the pair limped out through the sanctuary gates to begin their new life together.

We never saw them again but I'm sure they enjoyed a happy life together. It really was a match made in heaven.

❋ ❋ ❋

I should have studied for my coming exams, but there was always something more interesting to do. My schoolfriend, Jo, and I had started writing each other letters, which was ridiculous as we saw each other at school every day anyway. What was in those daily letters? I have no idea, I simply can't remember. I asked Jo just a few weeks ago if she could remember what we wrote about.

"No, I don't remember at all," she replied, casting her mind back more than forty years. "I just remember writing them, and getting them every day, and I remember they made me laugh. And they were a lot more interesting than revising."

Examination time arrived. Once again we sat in long silent rows in the gym.

"You may now turn your papers over and begin," said the invigilator.

I stared at the questions and began writing. If I failed these exams, and couldn't go to Teacher Training College, then what? I was furious with myself for not studying harder.

Straight after the exams came a time of relaxation, but also uncertainty. It was too late to study and nothing I did now could influence my 'A' Level results. Time would tell.

❋ ❋ ❋

"*Ach,* that's the postman."

"I can't look," I said, a bag of nerves.

"I'll see if the results have arrived."

166

My mother scooped up the envelopes from the door mat and sifted through them.

"Yes, your 'A' Level results are here."

"I can't look."

"*Ach,* shall I open the envelope for you?"

"Yes, please. I can't look."

I was sitting on the stairs, my hands covering my face. Now was the moment of truth. If I'd failed, as I deserved to, my dream of a teaching career was over.

"Well?"

I peeped through my fingers, trying to read my mother's expression as she unfolded the letter.

"You passed them all!"

"I did? Are you sure?"

My future was mapped out. I would become a teacher.

※ ※ ※

Autumn was on the way. At school, we'd already said our goodbyes and signed our names on each other's uniforms. We would be scattering to universities and training colleges the length and breadth of Britain.

It was my last day at the animal sanctuary. I'd given up pretending not to watch for Tony amongst the visitors. I always searched for him in the sea of faces when the sanctuary gates opened to let visitors in. I'd hold my breath, but Tony never came. He promised he'd come to say goodbye, but he couldn't even be bothered to do that.

"Well, Nig-Nog, it's just you and me today," I said, leaning down and rubbing his cheek the way he loved.

"Puuurrp!"

A wave of sadness rippled over me.

"I'm really, really going to miss you, you know."

"And I'm going to miss you, Vicky."

I jumped. I knew that voice.

Has he come back to say goodbye after all?

Slowly, slowly, heart somersaulting, I turned to see who had spoken.

"I'm so sorry, Vicky, I just didn't know how to tell you," said Tony.

I stared at him, speechless. Was *this* my Tony? Where was the long, dirty blond hair and bushy moustache? Where were the beads? Where was the psychedelic shirt and bell-bottom jeans? Where was Tony the Hippy?

In front of me stood a clean-shaven lad with short, neat hair and Marks and Spencer clothes. He didn't look unattractive, but this wasn't the Tony I'd fallen for. In that instant, I was cured.

"I came to say goodbye," said Tony.

"Goodbye?" I echoed. "You needn't have bothered. Really."

And I meant it.

Tony had done me a favour. Now I could look forward to my exciting future without regrets, without that ache in my heart that Tony had left. I was free.

I *was* upset, but not about Tony. I was upset about leaving Nig-Nog, and all the other animals, and Big Denise, and all the wonderful friends I had made at the animal sanctuary.

I cleared out my locker for the last time, and found a little folded note that had just been pushed through the crack in the locker door. I unfolded it.

> *Vicky, I hope you've forgiven me. I've missed you a lot these past weeks and you are always in my thoughts. I really hope we can get together during the holidays and pick up where we left off. Please get in touch.*
> *All my love,*
> *T xxx*

I screwed up the note in my hand and walked over to the wastepaper bin. I dropped the crumpled paper in.

No, I said to myself. *No, that's not going to happen.*

❄ ❄ ❄

"*Ach,* are you sure you've got everything?"

"Yes, I think so."

"It's going to be a long drive, you know."

It was 1973, I was eighteen years old and we were heading to West Sussex. The journey would take most drivers a couple of hours, but this was my mother driving Ivy. It would most likely take four or five hours, and we'd packed a picnic.

"Right, off we go!" shouted my mother, turning the ignition key and crunching Ivy's gears alarmingly.

My father had made sure that Ivy was facing the right way; my mother still hadn't mastered the art of reversing. I took a last look at my childhood home over my shoulder and held tight as Ivy bucked away.

The future looked bright.

Epilogue

The next section of my life, covering college days, marriage and children, remains unrecorded as yet, a project for the future perhaps. Is it possible to write a sequel to a prequel?

My sister left university with a decent degree, but no real idea of what she wanted to do. Already bitten by the travel bug, she worked in an Israeli kibbutz for a while. The Yom Kippur War began with a surprise Arab attack on Israel on Saturday 6th October 1973 and my sister was airlifted out of the kibbutz. There was no time to pack possessions, she and her colleagues had to escape in just the clothes they were wearing.

Unperturbed, she then went to work in Cyprus until July 1974 when Turkish forces suddenly invaded the country. Once again, my sister was airlifted out. Once again, there was no time to pack possessions. She and her colleagues escaped in just the clothes they were wearing.

"*Ach,*" said my mother, looking over her shoulder as though expecting to spot troops amassing in the shadows behind the compost heap. "I'm a bit nervous of her coming back to Wareham. She seems to attract wars."

My sister went on to carve out a career working all over the world for the Voluntary Services Overseas (VSO), the British equivalent to the Peace Corps, and language development projects. We blame her for starting the revolution in Iran two months after she began work there. She eventually married a fellow free spirit.

My brother followed in my father's footsteps and joined the Army for a while, before working for himself. He is married and has three sons.

My mother and father both died in 1993, within three months of each other.

Auntie Jean and Uncle Frank passed away recently after some illness. Annabel, now the mother of two boys, returned to Wareham to nurse her parents and is still there.

My schoolfriend, Jo, married a screenwriter. The couple and their two young daughters moved to Los Angeles for a while. Disillusioned with La-La Land, they returned to Dorset and the girls attended Parkstone Grammar School, just like their mother had done.

I don't know if Janice Parry ended up marrying my crush, Barry. Neither do I have any idea what happened to Tony the Hippy.

Mrs Cox and Jeannie passed away a long time ago, but not before they had raised a shedload more money for the charity, Guide Dogs for the Blind.

I thrived at Teacher Training College and enjoyed living in West Sussex. I married and had children. Living yards from the sea was wonderful, even though our local beach couldn't be compared with beautiful Studland or Sandbanks, or the other fabulous Dorset beaches that were part of my childhood.

Fast forward thirty years or more. Life in West Sussex had been good. Our children had grown up and flown away, and Joe was on the verge of retirement.

But at the age when most people want to take on less, I decided to do the complete opposite and turn our lives upside down. I nagged poor long-suffering Joe into moving to a tiny, remote village in the Spanish mountains.

What happened next is told in *Chickens, Mules and Two Old Fools* and the sequels.

If you enjoyed *One Young Fool in Dorset*, I would be forever grateful if you would consider leaving a review. Thank you!

Preview of Chickens, Mules and Two Old Fools

1
The Five Year Plan

"Hello?"

"This is Kurt."

"Oh! Hello, Kurt. How are you?"

"I am vell. The papers you vill sign now. I haf made an appointment vith the Notary for you May 23rd, 12 o'clock."

"Right, I'll check the flights and…" but he had already hung up.

Kurt, our German estate agent, was the type of person one obeyed without question. So, on May 23rd, we found ourselves back in Spain, seated round a huge polished table in the Notary's office. Beside us sat our bank manager holding a briefcase stuffed with bank notes.

ቋቋቋ

Nine months earlier, we had never met Kurt. Nine months earlier, Joe and I lived in an ordinary house, in an ordinary Sussex town. Nine months earlier we had ordinary jobs and expected an ordinary future.

Then, one dismal Sunday, I decided to change all that.

"**…heavy showers are expected to last through the Bank Holiday weekend and into next week. Temperatures are struggling to reach 14 degrees…**"

August, and the weather-girl was wearing a coat, sheltering under an umbrella. June had been wet, July wetter. I sighed, stabbing the 'off' button on the remote control before she could depress me further. Agh! Typical British weather.

My depression changed to frustration. The private thoughts that had been tormenting me so long returned. Why should we put up with it? Why not move? Why not live in my beloved Spain where the sun always shines?

I walked to the window. Raindrops like slug trails trickled down the windowpane. Steely clouds hung low, heavy with more rain, smothering the town. Sodden litter sat drowning in the gutter.

"Joe?" He was dozing, stretched out on the sofa, mouth slightly open.

"Joe, I want to talk to you about something."

Poor Joe, my long-suffering husband. His gangly frame was sprawled out, newspaper slipping from his fingers. He was utterly relaxed, blissfully unaware that our lives were about to change course.

How different he looked in scruffy jeans compared with his usual crisp uniform. But to me, whatever he wore, he was always the same, an officer and a gentleman. Nearing retirement from the Forces, I knew he was looking forward to a tension-free future, but the television weather-girl had galvanised me into action. The metaphorical bee in my bonnet would not be stilled. It buzzed and grew until it became a hornet demanding attention.

House in England

"Huh? What's the matter?" His words were blurred with sleep, his eyes still closed. Rain beat a tattoo on the window pane.

"Joe? Are you listening?"

"Uhuh..."

"When you retire, I want us to sell up and buy a house in Spain." Deep breath.

There. The bomb was dropped. I had finally admitted my longing. I wanted to abandon England with its ceaseless rain. I wanted to move permanently to Spain.

Sleep forgotten, Joe pulled himself upright, confusion in his blue eyes as he tried to read my expression.

"Vicky, what did you say just then?" he asked, squinting at me.

"I want to go and live in Spain."

"You can't be serious."

"Yes, I am."

Of course it wasn't just the rain. I had plenty of reasons, some vague, some more solid.

I presented my pitch carefully. Our children, adults now, were scattered round the world; Scotland, Australia and London. No grandchildren yet on the horizon and Joe only had a year before he retired. Then we would be free as birds to nest where we pleased.

And the cost of living in Spain would be so much lower. Council tax a fraction of what we usually paid, cheaper food, cheaper houses... The list went on.

Joe listened closely and I watched his reactions. Usually, *he* is the impetuous one, not me. But I was well aware that his retirement fantasy was being threatened. His dream of lounging all day in his dressing-gown, writing his book and diverting himself with the odd mathematical problem was being exploded.

"Hang on, Vicky, I thought we had it all planned? I thought you would do a few days of supply teaching if you wanted, while I start writing my book." Joe absentmindedly scratched his nether regions. For once I ignored his infuriating habit; I was in full flow.

"But imagine writing in Spain! Imagine sitting outside in the shade of a grapevine and writing your masterpiece."

Outside, windscreen wipers slapped as cars swept past, tyres sending up plumes of filthy water. Joe glanced out of the window at the driving rain and I sensed I had scored an important point.

"Why don't you write one of your famous lists?" he suggested, only half joking.

I am well known for my lists and records. Inheriting the record- keeping gene from my father, I can't help myself. I make a note of the weather every day, the temperature, the first snowdrop, the day the ants fly, the exchange rate of the euro, everything. I make shopping lists, separate ones for each shop. I make To Do lists and 'Joe, will you please' lists. I make packing lists before holidays. I even make lists of lists. My nickname at work was Schindler.

So I set to work and composed what I considered to be a killer pitch:

- Sunny weather
- Cheap houses
- Live in the country
- Miniscule council tax
- Friendly people
- Less crime
- No heating bills
- Cheap petrol
- Wonderful Spanish food
- Cheap wine and beer
- Could get satellite TV so you won't miss English football
- Much more laid-back life style
- Could afford house big enough for family and visitors to stay
- No TV licence

- Only short flight to UK
- Might live longer because Mediterranean diet is healthiest in the world

When I ran dry, I handed the list to Joe. He glanced at it and snorted.

"I'm going to make a coffee," he said, but he took my list with him. He was in the kitchen a long time.

When he came out, I looked up at him expectantly. He ignored me, snatched a pen and scribbled on the bottom of the list. Satisfied, he threw it on the table and left the room. I grabbed it and read his additions. He'd pressed so hard with the pen that he'd nearly gone through the paper.

Joe had written:

- CAN'T SPEAK SPANISH!
- TOO MANY FLIES!
- *MOVING HOUSE IS THE PITS!*

For weeks we debated, bouncing arguments for and against like a game of ping pong. Even when we weren't discussing it, the subject hung in the air between us, almost tangible. Then one day, (was it a coincidence that it was raining yet again?) Joe surprised me.

"Vicky, why don't you book us a holiday over Christmas, and we could just take a look."

The hug I gave him nearly crushed his ribs.

"Hang on!" he said, detaching himself and holding me at arm's length. "What I'm trying to say is, well, I'm willing to compromise."

"What do you mean, 'compromise'?"

"How about if we look on it as a five year plan? We don't sell this house, just rent it out. Okay, we could move to Spain, but not necessarily for ever. At the end of five years, we can make up our minds whether to come back to England or stay out there. I'm happy to try it for five years. What do you think?"

I turned it over in my mind. Move to Spain, but look on it as a sort of project? Actually, it seemed rather a good idea. In fact, a perfect compromise.

Joe was watching me. "Well? Agreed?"

"Agreed..." It was a victory of sorts. A Five Year Plan. Yes, I saw the sense in that. Anything could happen in five years.

"Well, go on, then. Book a holiday over Christmas and we'll take it from there."

So I logged onto the Internet and booked a two week holiday in Almería.

Why Almería? Well, we already knew the area quite well as this would be our fourth visit. And I considered this part of Andalucía to be perfect. Only two and a half hours flight from London, guaranteed sunshine, friendly people and jaw-dropping views. It ticked all my boxes. Joe agreed cautiously that the area could be ideal.

So the destination was decided, but what type of home in Spain would we want? Our budget was reduced because we weren't going to sell our English house. We'd have to find something cheap.

On previous visits, I'd hated all the houses we'd noticed in the resorts. Mass produced boxes on legoland estates, each identical, each characterless and overlooking the next. No, I knew what I really wanted: a house we could do up, with views and space, preferably in an unspoiled Spanish village.

Unlike Joe, I've always been obsessed with houses. I was the driving force and it was the hard climb up the English property ladder that allowed us even to contemplate moving abroad. In the past few years, we had bought a derelict house, improved and sold it, making a good profit. So we bought another and repeated the process. It was gruelling work. We both had other careers, but it was well worth the effort. Now we could afford to rent out our home in England and still buy a modest house in Spain.

"If we do decide to move out there," said Joe, "and we buy an old place to do up, it's not going to be like doing up houses in England. Everything's going to be different there."

How right he was.

ጿጿጿ

Like a child, I yearned for that Christmas to come. I couldn't wait to set foot on Spanish soil again. We arrived, and although Christmas lights decorated the airport, it was warm enough to remove our jackets. Before long, we had found our hotel and settled in.

The next morning, we hired a little car. Joe, having finally accepted the inevitable, was happy to drive into the mountains in search of The House. We had two weeks to find it.

Yet again the mountains seduced us. The endless blue sky where birds of prey wheeled lazily. The neat orchards splashed with bright oranges and lemons. The secret, sleepy villages nestled into valleys. Even the roads, narrow, treacherous and winding, couldn't break the spell that Andalucía cast over us.

Daily, we drove through whitewashed villages where little old ladies dressed in black stopped sweeping their doorsteps to watch us pass. We waved at farmers working in their fields, the dry dust swirling in irritated clouds from their labours. We paused to allow goat-herds to pass with their flocks, the lead goat's bell clanging bossily as the herd followed, snatching mouthfuls of vegetation on the run.

Although we hadn't yet found The House, we were positive we'd found the area we wanted to live in.

One day we drove into a village that clung to the steep mountainside by its fingernails. We entered a bar that was buzzing with activity. It was busy and the air heavy with smoke. The white-aproned bartender looked us up and down and jerked his head in greeting. No smile, just a nod.

Joe found a rocky wooden table by the window with panoramic views and we settled ourselves, soaking in the atmosphere. Four old men played cards at the next table. A heated debate was taking place between another group. I caught the words 'Barcelona' and 'Real Madrid'. Most of the bar's customers were male.

Grumpy, the bartender, wiped his hands on his apron and approached our table, flicking off imaginary crumbs from the surface with the back of his hand. He had a splendid moustache which concealed any expression he may have had, and made communication difficult.

"Could we see the menu, please?" asked Joe in his best phrase book Spanish.

Grumpy shook his head and snorted. It seemed there was no menu.

"No *importa*," said Joe. "It doesn't matter."

Using a combination of sign

Grumpy's Garlic Mushrooms Tapa
Champiñones al Ajillo
Serves 4

50ml (2 fl oz) extra virgin olive oil
250g (8oz) fresh mushrooms (sliced)
4-6 cloves of garlic (chopped or sliced)
3 tablespoons dry Spanish sherry
2 tablespoons lemon juice
Large pinch of dried chili flakes
Large pinch of paprika
Salt, freshly ground pepper
Chopped parsley to garnish

Method
• Heat the oil in a frying pan and fry the mushrooms over a high heat for 2 or 3 minutes. Stir constantly.
• Lower the heat and add the garlic, lemon juice, sherry, salt and pepper.
• For a milder flavour you can leave it at that if you like. But if you like a few 'fireworks', now is the time to add the dried chili and paprika as well.
• Cook for another 5 minutes or so until the garlic and mushrooms have softened, then remove from the heat.
• Sprinkle with chopped parsley and divide up into pre-heated little dishes.
• Serve with plenty of fresh, crusty bread to mop up the seriously garlicky juices.

Note: Tapa means 'lid' or 'cover' in Spanish. It's thought that the name originally came from the practice of placing slices of meat on top of a sherry glass, to keep out flies. The meat, often ham or chorizo, was characteristically salty, inducing thirst. Bartenders saw this and began serving a variety of tapas which increased alcohol sales. Thus a new tradition was born.

language and impatient grunts, Grumpy took our order but our meal was destined to be a surprise. A basket of bread was slammed onto the table, followed by two plates of food. Garlic mushrooms - delicious. We cleaned our plates and leaned back, digesting our food and the surroundings. In typical Spanish fashion, the drinkers at the bar bellowed at each other as though every individual had profound hearing problems.

"We're running out of time," said Joe. "We can carry on gallivanting around the countryside, but we aren't going to find anything. I very much doubt we'll find a house this holiday."

Suddenly, clear as cut crystal, the English words, "Oh, bugger! Where are my keys?" floated above the Spanish hubbub.

If you'd like to keep abreast of my life,
do join me on Facebook.

https://www.facebook.com/VictoriaTwead
(friend requests welcome)

Contact the Author and Links

Email: TopHen@VictoriaTwead.com
(emails welcome)

Facebook: https://www.facebook.com/VictoriaTwead
(friend requests welcome)

Website: www.VictoriaTwead.com

Free Stuff and Village Updates newsletter
http://www.victoriatwead.com/Free-Stuff/

Twitter: @VictoriaTwead
and
@StephenFrysCat

Chickens, Mules and Two Old Fools book trailer:
http://youtu.be/1s9KbJEmrHs

Acknowledgements

Most importantly, thanks must go yet again to **my loyal readers**. Thank you for taking the time to read my scribblings and HUGE thanks to those of you who have taken the trouble to leave reviews. Authors love reviews more than wine or chocolate and I read and appreciate every comment.

Thanks to **Nick Saltmer** who painted the cover picture of Wareham quay. This is the fifth cover he has painted for me and I cannot decide which I love best.

Thank you to the members of the **We Love Memoirs** Facebook group. You are an amazing bunch and not a day goes by when I don't pop in for a chat and laugh.

Come and join us - you'll get a warm welcome!
https://www.facebook.com/groups/welovememoirs)

Photo Acknowledgements
- Dorchester Hospital by Sarah Smith, CC BY-SA 2.0 via Wikimedia Commons
- "Corfe Castle 57" by Chin tin tin - Own work. Licensed under CC BY 3.0 via Wikimedia Commons
- "Steam Train, Corfe Castle Station 1" Personal photograph taken by Mick Knapton at en.wikipedia. Licensed under CC BY-SA 3.0 via Wikimedia Commons
- Old Clavell Tower - www.landmark.org.uk
- New Clavell Tower - Copyright Tony Atkin and licensed for reuse under the Creative Commons Licence
- Durdle Door - Copyright Gwyn Jones and licensed for reuse under the Creative Commons Licence.
- Cerne Abbas Giant - Copyright Maurice D Budden and licensed for reuse under the Creative Commons Licence.
- The Shell House, Southbourne Overcliff Drive, Southbourne, Bournemouth, Dorset "Sunny South" Real Photo by Dearden & Wade, Ltd., Bournemouth..
- Talbot Heath https://avenuesltd.wordpress.com/2013/01/07/talbot-heath-school-bournemouth/
- "Max Gate Dorchester" by Pierre Terre. Licensed under CC BY-SA 2.0 via Wikimedia Commons
- Brecon Beacons "Veil of Snow - Sgwd yr Eira" by Saffron Blaze - Own work. Via Wikimedia Commons
- Baby hedgehog Credit Photo (creative commons): Last Human Gateway
- Gannet - By Amateria1121 (Own work) [CC BY-SA 3.0 (http://creativecommons.org/licenses/by-sa/3.0)], via Wikimedia Commons

Books by Victoria Twead

The Old Fools Series
- Chickens, Mules and Two Old Fools (Wall Street Journal bestseller)
- Two Old Fools ~ Olé!
- Two Old Fools on a Camel (New York Times bestseller x 3)
- Two Old Fools in Spain Again

Also by Victoria Twead
- How to Write a Bestselling Memoir
- Mouth-Watering Spanish Recipes
- Morgan and the Martians ~ A Comedy Play-Script for Kids

Ant Press Books

If you enjoyed this book, you may also enjoy these Ant Press memoirs:

Chickens, Mules and Two Old Fools by Victoria Twead (Wall Street Journal Top 10 bestseller)
Two Old Fools ~ Olé! byVictoria Twead
Two Old Fools on a Camel by Victoria Twead (New York Times bestseller)
Two Old Fools in Spain Again by Victoria Twead

Into Africa with 3 Kids, 13 Crates and a Husband by Ann Patras

Paw Prints in Oman: Dogs, Mogs and Me by Charlotte Smith (New York Times bestseller)

Joan's Descent into Alzheimer's by Jill Stoking

The Girl Behind the Painted Smile: My battle with the bottle by Catherine Lockwood

The Coconut Chronicles: Two Guys, One Caribbean Dream House by Patrick Youngblood

Fat Dogs and French Estates ~ Part I by Beth Haslam
Fat Dogs and French Estates ~ Part II by Beth Haslam

Made in the USA
San Bernardino, CA
13 June 2016